This sweet ass journal belongs to: _____

If found, please contact: _____

SWEET ASS JOURNAL
TO DEVELOP
YOUR
HAPPINESS
MUSCLE

in 100 days

Disclaimer

The information provided within this publication is for general informational purposes only, even when used to battle or **kiss** intergalactic space aliens. While we try to keep the information up-to-date and correct, there are no representations or warranties, express or implied, about the completeness, accuracy, reliability, suitability or availability with respect to the information, products, services, or related graphics contained in this publication for any purpose. Any use of this information is at your own risk.

The methods describe within this guide and journal are the author's personal thoughts which come from a creative sinkhole in a galaxy full of smiles and corn dogs. They are not intended to be a definitive set of instructions for this project. You may discover there are other methods and materials to accomplish the same end result. You may also discover that the author's methods do not generate the same results for you. Either way you're still a champion and **my** (possibly the author) inner warrior salutes you. Keep flexing.

The author does not assume and hereby disclaims any liability to any party for any loss, damage, or disruption caused by errors or omissions, whether such errors or omissions result from accident, negligence, space gremlins, or any other cause. This journal is most effective when fast food, sitting on your **sweet ass**, and reality television are avoided, which also results in fresher undies and more mental clarity. Put your game face on.

In short, if you wish to apply ideas contained in this publication, you are taking full responsibility for your actions. Bottoms up.

ISBN-13: 978-1543276497
Designed by Heath Armstrong
Edited by Lily Ann Fouts
Cover Art by Riley Armstrong

Published by Heath Armstrong

For inquiries about permissions for reproducing parts of this guide and journal, please e-mail heath@fistpumps.com

For more information, visit the author's website at www.heatharmstrong.com

Dedication

To Arlonious Bologna Armstrong, for pissing all over my old journal and forcing me to use a plain notebook instead, which became the first template of this project.

And, for teaching the world how to be happy and calm no matter what life presents, except for when the mailman comes. You taught me to give zero fucks. Your stoicism will always be with me.

SWEET ASS CONTENTS

You can download and print the journal template files at home by visiting
www.sweetassjournal.com/bonus

Join our Live Q&A's with Sweet Ass People through the bonus link above - hosted in our private Facebook group.

Also Check Out:

The Sweet Ass Domination Deck
www.ragecreate.com

The Never Stop Peaking Podcast
www.HeathArmstrong.com/podcast
iTunes | Stitcher

Introduction

Life is gorgeous, but it can also be a grindhouse poo-fest if your mind is in the wrong place. There is magic in creation, in all forms of nature, and in every moment, but there is no denying that sometimes we all get stuck in the shitter. Regardless of how we are feeling, we wake up every morning strapped to a giant mysterious rock, parading in an orbital path at 67,000 miles per hour around a giant ball of fire. When did you last spend a moment in gratitude for this miraculous existence?

As multitasking modern maniac humans, we lose touch with the beauty in the world and become puppets to resistance, stress, depression, and desire. We experience hopelessness, confusion, and loneliness in a world where all eyes follow a media which endlessly spews hate, violence, and suffering.

Shame on those media weenies! I have glowing news! No one is in charge of your mindset except you. You can replace all your fears and darkness with happiness and freedom if you simply commit to a daily practice of awakening the magic within you.

I was in a dark and eerie place when I first made a commitment to change. I worked 10+ hours per day in a career I despised to buy junk I didn't need to impress people I didn't like. In other words, I was living the traditional American rollercoaster of life. I had over $20,000 in personal debt (not including my mortgage which I couldn't afford) and a routine of immeasurable drinking to numb the thoughts of my situation. I even woke up one morning on my garage floor with a nose bleed and an empty bottle of whiskey sitting upright on my doorstep. My car sat in the middle of the front lawn with the engine running. Although this was an extremely dark time in my life, it was the rock-bottom moment that led to the transformation of the person I have become now. Sometimes we have to go down before we rise up.

Today, I share this moment with you from my deep heart and a level of happiness and freedom beyond comprehension. I feel immeasurable gratitude to have you join me on this journey. Everyone is unique in their mind, heart, and situation, but one thing is absolute: progress is the direct result of persistence.

If you stick to your commitment to make progress, you will always make progress. It's as simple as that.

When I made my commitment, I realized I had two choices:

1. Make progress towards the life of my dreams.
2. Suffer and die.

As extreme as this sounds, it's the same commitment we all must make if we wish to triumph over conformity and create the sporadic and adventurous life we love. We must choose to be better, and then act to bring the vision to reality.

Instead of suffering all day in a miserable job that we despise and wishing away our days and weeks for nights and weekends, we should dream of a life of fulfillment, travel, adventures, experience, creation, and purpose. I dreamed of owning my own creative business, having the ability to work from anywhere in the world, paying off all my debt, moving to the Pacific Northwest, and creating with passion daily. I dreamed of happiness in each moment, and the ability to freely choose how to spend all moments of MY life.

My dream is now reality. My vision has manifested.

I am no different than you, which means you can also create the life you love even if you are in a black hole of doubt and resistance. I am no smarter than you, I only discovered the portal and put in the work. We are reflections of each other at different stages of life.

In just 2 1/2 years:

- I spent 150+ hours interviewing over 100 creative masterminds and entrepreneurs on bringing dreams to life. (You can view and stream the full list of interviews at *www.heatharmstrong.com/interviews*)
- I sold my house and everything I owned to eliminate distractions, pay off ALL my debt, and discover meaning.
- I retired my 'career' for full-time location-independence, freedom, and travel.
- I built an automated $60k/month (MRR) e-commerce business which is 95% automated. I "work" one hour a day on this business.
- I moved to the Pacific Northwest as my fiancée and I always dreamed to do.
- I am my own boss, and I allow myself 365 vacation days/year.
- Every day is a Saturday.

When I retrace my steps to this point, all I see is my will to make progress. Because I refuse to quit, no matter how dark and hard the situation, I always end up in the direction I am working towards. I continuously create my vision by simply choosing to create it.

When I started interviewing 100+ brilliant authors, directors, travel junkies, artists, philanthropists, and world-changers from across the globe, I was scared beyond reason to even approach these "successful" people. My lack of authority, credentials, or confidence in my ability to engage on the same level weakened me to the point of doubt, anxiety, and even nervous vomiting.

My second interview was with Hollywood director Sohrab Mirmont, an interview I believed I was about 1% likely to convert. When he said yes, I felt a rush of unbelievable accomplishment even though the interview hadn't even happened yet. It gave me all the confidence I needed to surge through my doubt and have faith in the goodwill of others.

In the world of successful and free people, everyone REALLY does want to help each other. This shared, common energy sparks the magic within anyone who is willing. Be willing.

Soon enough, I experienced an awakening of my mind, heart, and outlook on life. My fear recessed, my energy grew, and I ached for more interviews. The interviews became fuel for my drive towards freedom, and I dissected and studied each interview like a scientist. I no longer sought ways to ignore and numb my situation. I embraced it, took action, and made progress in my life.

I thought, if all these people can create a life of freedom and happiness, then there must be light in the world after all! Right?

But HOW do I create this life for myself? How do others create this life?

I shifted the focus of my conversations to pinpoint this curiosity. With the birth of each new interview, I began noticing extreme similarities in the mental and physical practices, habits, and strategies of these happy and free masterminds. Then, I tested each of them in my own life like a guinea pig on speed. Over time, I sifted through all the fundamentals that worked wonders for me, and I began reviewing and practicing each daily.

I started by using The Five-Minute Journal for gratitude, happiness, and reflection, and I even had the creator, UJ Ramdas, on my podcast for an interview on how to hack your happiness. *(You can hear that interview on* **www.heatharmstrong.com/interviews***)* If you haven't used his journal, it's another beautiful option and was my go-to for two years.

As I continued my interviews and the dissection of all the fundamentals, strategies, and habits of these awesome successful people, more and more practices started falling into my journal routine. Before I knew it, I carried around five different journals, each for a different purpose. Keeping up with all of them became difficult. Opening all the different covers felt overwhelming. One time, I left a section behind at a coffee shop, and it was like Armageddon in my head. I have some weird thoughts. The idea of someone reading my thoughts, or even checking out the drawings of my booty, got me all hot and bothered. Wait, I mean nervous and stressed... NOT hot and bothered. The booty pictures I can't explain.

Anyway, I'm a little embarrassed it took me this long, but eventually, the creative gods blessed me with the idea to put the pieces into an all-in-one journal. Today, this practice has evolved into a personal journey of daily awakening, and it's a sacred part of both my mornings and nights. Without the practice, and the experience of creating the practice, I would still be in a very dark place.

Taking Charge

To be successful, first acknowledge you need to make changes. Then be relentless in manifesting these changes. My goal with this sweet ass journal is to help you stay focused on the magic of life in the moment, so that you may utilize all moments to efficiently create and sustain a life of freedom, happiness, and purpose forever.

If you take only one step toward completing a section of this journal daily, then EVERY day you are moving in the direction of your vision, personal development, and ultimate happiness and freedom.

Even though I designed this journal to optimize your happiness, I also aim for it to be a shortcut to kickstart and track your magical journey. The journal is not meant to be overwhelming, so don't feel anxious or stressed if you miss a few sections or days. I fall off track often, but it's always there to pick back up when I need it the most.

In the following sections of this sweet ass journal, you are going to learn the power of practicing gratitude, brainstorming ideas, focusing, gifting, minimizing, celebrating, planning, affirming, meditating and reflecting.

PART 1:

SETTING THE STAGE

Becoming Something More

As with any journey in life, we should aim for something more. Every moment of every day, we should progress toward a happier, healthier, and more valuable self. Take action during your days to ensure that you are a better person every night than you were when you woke up that morning.

Use this journal persistently, and you may notice some magical changes similar to everything I and the creative masterminds that I interviewed around the world have experienced. I am not suggesting that by filling out a page of this journal every once in awhile, you will become superhuman with the answers to all of life. However, if you use this journal with the fire for freedom that burns within you, you will learn how to:

- Set a vision for your 100-day transformation. Stop the guesswork and know where you actually want to be by the end of 100 days!
- Kickstart your days with big smiles and a breakfast of gratitude. Wrap your brain around positive vibes to shape the rest of your day.
- Identify and dominate your most valuable daily actions. No more wasted time on meaningless goober tasks.
- Become a master of brainstorming ideas, some of which will change your life and become your creative masterpieces!
- Eliminate emotional and physical distractions and surround yourself with value. Less is more.

- Bring back and sustain the warm fuzzy feeling you had as a child. Remember that sweet ass feeling?
- Become what you think about. Bring your visions to reality!
- Use your breath as a superpower by discovering the magic of mindfulness.
- Reflect upon and celebrate your progress to optimize motivation and excitement. Keep the momentum going so you don't just stop at 100 days.
- Beef up your happiness muscle to body-slam resistance and build your freedom empire!

It's almost time to start your sweet ass transformation, but first, let's set a vision for the ride!

A Quick Note on Resistance Gremlins

You may see this phrase throughout the journal and in most of my work, so I suppose it deserves a brief explanation. We experience the monster of resistance in our lifelong battle to create our freedom and happiness empires. Some of the more common forms of resistance are fear, stress, anxiety, and procrastination. Brilliant authors and philosophers have dissected resistance in their works since the beginning of literacy (Steven Pressfield's The War of Art being my favorite), and there is good reason for this. Resistance is the enemy of creation. If we can identify it and suppress it, we can create magic.

When we resist, we conform to the death of creation - the death of ourselves. When we create, we destroy resistance. Obviously, to manifest a life of pure happiness and freedom, we must create it. Therefore, we must destroy resistance.

Everyone experiences resistance, but not everyone can identify the beast. It can creep into life in disguise as comfort, assurance, and even family/friends. So, it's impeccably important to be able to identify resistance, and then take all actions necessary to obtain, suppress, and slaughter it!

If we attach "gremlin" to the back of resistance, it makes it easier for us to understand that resistance is a real living energy of evil that lives to dismantle our creations and hinder our progress. Then, we can personify anything that stands in our way by attaching a gremlin face and body to it. In my world, there are email gremlins, Facebook gremlins, alcohol gremlins, weather gremlins, sleep gremlins, exercise gremlins, focus gremlins, and even travel gremlins! These nasty little goons can show up anywhere, anytime, in any form, and it's not only humorous to envision them with gremlin heads, but it directly helps to keep the focus on identifying and destroying anything that stands in the way of our persistence and personal creative development.

Resistance gremlins are your enemy. Keep your weapons sharp and make those little bastards pee in their undies! Give them wedgies and bully them! Steal and eat their lunches!

Kickstarting the Habit & Tracking Momentum

Your new journal is laid out in 100 days and nights to make it incredibly easy to track your progress. Because there are 100 days of journaling, each page represents 1% of 100%. Therefore, if you complete your journal on day one, you are 1% to completing your 100 days of developing your happiness muscle! If you wrap up entry 98, you'll be 98% finished with pumping that happiness muscle into full shape! And I can attest, each day that you complete will be a step toward ultimate happiness and freedom. You can always see what percent you have completed by checking the bottom right-hand corner of the journal.

Did I accomplish my two main freedom actions today? ☺ ☺ ☹

Did I give a gift and/or minimize? ☺ ☺ ☹

What was it and how did it feel? _____

I meditated for .... minutes today and I felt: _____

You are   3 % done with developing your happiness muscle :)

Sweet Ass Freedom Buds

Before you start this journey, it's important to visualize who you wish to become in this process.

By creating a vision, you are setting a focus for where you are heading in life. If you follow the direction of your vision, you will create the life of your dreams. If you fail to create your own vision, others will make your vision for you by placing ads, commercials, billboards, religions, politics, traditions, and spray-tanning machines around you. Do yourself a monstrous favor and define your future without these outside influences!

Since you have this journal in your hand, you are already taking action to building the future you. Below, write down the three freedom buds (AKA visions, goals, or dreams) that you wish to bloom between now and the 100 awesome days of this ride. Aim high! Coming up short on a big scary goal is better than accomplishing one with minimal effort. You will come to a point where you will achieve one (or all) of your visions before the 100-day journaling is complete. Celebrate! Treat yourself to a super tasty night out! Then, keep hustling toward your other visions and set a new one in place of the one you have already brought to reality.

Here are some examples that I have used (or am currently using) to get your mind jogging:

- Travel to Africa and help out a non-profit for a month
- Write the outline and rough draft of my first book
- Create a side business that makes $300 extra per month
- Run my first half marathon
- Call a new family member or friend every day
- Increase my sales accounts at work by 20%
- Become fluent in Spanish
- Sell the house and move to the Pacific Northwest
- Hire and train virtual assistants to help scale Amazon business to $100k/month in sales

Your turn!

My sweet ass freedom buds are:

- ....
- ....
- ....

Now, rewrite them so that when you repeat them out loud, it's as if they are happening, or they have already happened:

- I am in Africa helping out a non-profit for a month
- I finished the outline and rough draft of my first book
- I am making $374 extra per month from my side business
- I finished my first half marathon, and am training for a full marathon
- I chat with a friend or family member every day on the phone
- I have five new sales accounts that I picked up, 20% more than I had previously
- I speak fluent Spanish
- I sold my house, and I live in the Pacific Northwest
- I have a team of virtual assistants that helped me reach $105k in sales on Amazon in December

Your turn again!

My sweet ass freedom buds are:

- ....
- ....
- ....

By framing these in the present tense, you store a vision in your mind of what you aim to become. In the upcoming pages, you'll learn how to set and reflect on the most valuable freedom actions to complete each day toward realizing your freedom buds. Eventually, you will reach a day where your visions are a reality. I'm not promising that every vision you set will come true. If I wrote "I am brewing beer on the moon," it's likely that this vision wouldn't come true (yet). But if you set reasonable goals that you believe in and care about, and you work toward them every day through your freedom actions, you will eventually bring them to reality.

You can download and print a reminder of your freedom buds to post on your wall and keep you on track at **www.sweetassjournal.com/bonus**

By the way, it's also awesome to create an actual vision board with pictures of your future life on it. For example, on my vision board, I have the cover of this journal with the words "my journal" written across it. I also have a picture of a cabin on a lake with the words "my home" written across it. These are visions that I am currently bringing to life every day. I highly recommend that you make your own vision board because one day you will stand in front of it and realize that everything on your board has manifested. It's an awesome feeling.

The Mosaic Journal Layout

Everyone has a different style for journaling. Some people go looney tunes and black out the entire page with notes and ink, and others have a simple approach. Sometimes I write huge and lowercase like I never made it out of first grade, and other times I write neat, small, and in all caps. Sometimes I even draw my ideas rather than writing them. It all depends on our energy level and creative mood at the moment.

Because we are all unique in our approach and there is no wrong way to journal, I (with the help of the creative eye of Jacqueline du Plessis) decided on a different layout for the pages. Instead of using a traditional and fixed horizontal line layout, which can actually make us feel overwhelmed if we don't fill all the lines, I laid out this journal in free space mosaic boxes. These boxes become best friends for those who love to write big, small, messy, clean, extensive and simple. They even act as a perfect canvas for all you creative doodlers out there! It does not matter if you write one-word answers, essays, or draw a picture of your booty! Don't be overwhelmed. Just move forward. ☺

PART 2:

OVERVIEW OF JOURNAL SECTIONS

AM and PM

I divided this journal into two sections: morning and evening. The morning section sets the right mood and energy for the day, while the evening section fosters reflection of our progress and optimizes our mindset before rest. There are no rules as to when you absolutely must fill the journal out. Sometimes I find myself filling out the night section on the following morning. The idea is to visit this journal twice a day, with time in between to awaken and build your freedom and happiness empire.

Remember, for guaranteed progress, honor persistence.

Quotes for Fist Pumping

At the top of every morning entry, there is a new quote or mantra for inspiration. Read these quotes out loud while you pump your fists in the air! Each one of them has a personal connection to helping me in my journey along the way, and I trust they will inspire and help you too!

MORNING SECTIONS
GUIDE

Big Cheese

What makes me smile?

To create a life of happiness is to fill life with smiles. By definition, a smile is "a pleased, kind, or amused facial expression." If smiles are the result of pleasure, kindness, amusement, and excitement, then a natural smile is a building block of long-term happiness. To increase our smiles, we must build our awareness of people, places, and things that bring us pleasure, kindness, amusement, and excitement. We must regularly pause and identify these things that make us happy. What easier way than taking a moment, every morning, to consider the root of our happiness?

By making this our first step in the morning, we kickstart our magical day, setting a positive tone and energy. We paint pleasure, kindness, amusement, and excitement into all interactions and experiences throughout the rest of the day.

I used to wake up angry, knowing that ten hours of my unfulfilling career lay in front of me. Because I flooded my mind with anger and discontent upon rising, I felt bitter and unaware of all the beautiful things that made me happy. As I went about my day, I centered on the negatives, so my experience was negative.

It works both ways!

You can reframe your mind to always think about happy things, infecting the rest of your day with a happy mindset!

As soon as I started focusing on the pure joys that brought happiness to my life, everything began to change. Because my awareness now centered on positives, the negative resistance gremlins got a kick in the ass out the door. Our brains are magical beasts that are a vital partner in our journey towards happiness and freedom. This simple morning routine is the seed to a much larger and longer life of pure happiness and freedom.

Remember, there is no wrong way to fill out your boxes! Keep it short, jam pack it full so it's running out of the box, or even do a little doodle of something that makes you smile. I'm a huge fan of drawing!

Examples of things that might make you smile:

Significant others, family, pizza parties, kayaking, unicorns, flowers, being alive, sex, dancing, sports, donkeys, meditation, colors, Jim Carey, sweet mullets, sloths, professional wrestling outfits, nature, the stars, scuba diving, giving gifts, bong rips, practical jokes, world travel, streaking, cartoons, skydiving, accomplishing goals, fist pumping, people watching at Phish concerts, Danny DeVito, connecting with new friends, a Friday night cocktail, working in your undies, a hot bath, creating something, snowboarding, giving compliments, receiving compliments, food trucks, beaches, Donald Trump's hair, and giving wedgies to resistance gremlins.

Start your mornings by thinking about what makes you smile, and your days will surely have a positive theme!

Attitude of Gratitude

What am I thankful for?

I know what you are thinking. Isn't this exactly like the section we just went over? Not quite.

Sure, all the things that make you smile can also be things you're thankful for, but not everything you are thankful for necessarily makes you smile.

Practicing gratitude, or being thankful, is about pausing and appreciating yourself, all that surrounds you, and every interaction and experience of life. It's about focusing on the blessings we do have, as opposed to fixating on what we don't. It's easy to degrade ourselves because we aren't pretty enough, smart enough, or as wealthy as others we know. But degrading yourself is just a mental version of shitting on yourself, and nobody wants to experience that (except one dude I know).

A simple daily act of awareness by logging all that we are thankful for, no matter how big or small, will help our minds focus on just how fortunate we are to be here now, just as we are. So many aspects of our life seem invisible because we are never required to think about them, yet without them, our lives wouldn't be even close to the same. The focus of this section is to not take anything for granted and to beef up our happiness muscle by focusing on the magical parts of life that hide in the dark and don't get enough credit (and no, I'm not talking about your rock-solid booty). Pack out this box with anything and everything you are thankful for. You can elaborate on why you're thankful for them, too.

Here are some examples from my journal:

- I am thankful for my hands which allow me to place my thoughts into writing
- I am thankful for my high-school teachers (particularly Mrs. Corey) who passed on knowledge to prepare me for life
- I am thankful that I can hold my pee in, because one day that may not be true
- I am thankful for the chores my mother forced me to do as a child because they defined my ability to be responsible
- I am thankful for my fears because they highlight my weaknesses, allowing me the opportunity to strengthen and grow in these areas

- I am thankful for my enemies because they help me identify the characteristics I don't want, which allows me to work toward improving those that I do
- I am thankful for technology, which allows me to make a living while traveling the world
- I am thankful for my senses which allow me to experience life, as not everyone has the same opportunity
- I am thankful for rain and vegetation, which allow all life forms to eat and survive
- I am thankful for my ancestors which all successfully reproduced to allow me the gift of life
- I am thankful for my structured education, as I know others are not as fortunate
- I am thankful for my dogs because they remind me that all things should make my tail wag
- I am thankful for each morning that I wake because every day is a bonus round

Wohoo! Now it's time to come up with some ideas to change your life!

Sweet Ass Ideas

As a kid, I was always scribbling down ideas! Ideas for awesome futuristic things that I wanted to create, plans to explore, or adventures to have. At some point in my youth, I stopped doing that, and I lost touch with my creative side. When I read James Altucher's Choose Yourself (an early staple in my quest for discovering freedom), I rediscovered the power of exercising ideas. Altucher calls this exercise "Idea Machine," and as I implemented it, I immediately came back in touch with the creativity from my childhood. To this day, every project and creation I am involved with is the result of an idea from this practice. Every idea is a new opportunity!

Write down ideas every day (or all day) to build up your idea muscle. As this muscle gets stronger, you will become more creative and efficient in brainstorming and problem-solving. Some of these ideas will become a special part of your journey to awaken your happiness and conquer your freedom.

I use this practice to brainstorm different areas of my life I'm currently working toward improving, but I don't focus too much on whether or not the ideas are quality, usable, or even realistic. As long as I show up and write down ideas, I'll eventually birth a golden nugget.

The quality of your ideas does not matter. It's about being persistent in generating them. There will be a mass of ideas that are poo-poo material, but there will also be sunshine and star material!

You will notice in your idea box that it says **"Sweet ass ideas for ...."** at the top. This blank is where you will enter the theme for your idea. Do your best to pick an area of your life, a project, or even a random topic, and then generate as many ideas as you can based on that theme in the box below. You can even use an idea you generated on a previous day as your theme, and then branch out from there!

For example, back in 2015, my theme for the day was "Ideas to save money hardcore," because my personal debt was a dagger to my freedom. Here are the ideas I generated:

Ideas to save $ hardcore:

- No more eating out
- No alcohol or bar tabs
- Create a savings game with Jacqueline (my coach) to sustain momentum while building my savings
- Set up a bank transfer of 15% from all paychecks to savings automatically, no matter what
- Rob 3 banks and open a premium restaurant where Marky Mark and the Funky Bunch permanently perform while everyone eats

- Set a goal to live off my current groceries for the next month. Use everything I have!
- Cut back podcasting services that I'm not fully using
- Create a gangster rap hit that goes viral and buy a gold chain to celebrate
- Sell furniture and other household items that I never use
- Ask myself before every purchase "Will this add absolute value to my life?"
- Pick up new sales accounts at work to increase commission
- Eat more rice, eggs, and other inexpensive but clean foods

That list ended up playing a massive role in my quest to eliminate my debt! Although some of the ideas were ridiculous, others helped lay the foundation for my financial freedom. I'll let you guess as to which is which.

Examples of other themes I have used:

- Ideas for making money on the side to help pay off debt
- Ideas for detoxing from social media to help my focus
- Ideas for songs to make on a gangster rap album
- Ideas for countries to visit before 2017
- Ideas to write blog posts about
- Ideas of trails to backpack this summer
- Ideas for being happier today
- Ideas for products to private label and sell online
- Ideas for things I can automate with a virtual assistant online
- Ideas for activities that make me sweat
- Ideas for sections on my personal website
- Ideas of awesome meals to make this week
- Ideas of things to get rid of or donate that are of no value to me
- Ideas for giving gifts
- Ideas for creating a journal to combine all my journals

I have several notebooks full of these idea lists, and it's magical when I read through them to see which ones came to life!

Freedom Actions

What are the two most valuable freedom actions I will take today to progress towards my vision, goals, and dream life?

By this point, you have already set your three sweet ass freedom buds for this 100 days of freedom journaling. The next step is taking daily actions that prioritize your freedom buds over all other to-do list mumbo jumbo. I use the word "actions" instead of "tasks" because "tasks" feels like a bad word to me. A task feels like a burden, and working toward freedom and happiness is NOT a burden. It's a rollercoaster of maniac action, and we all LOVE action because it's exciting!

It's no secret that being a goal-oriented person will greatly increase your ability to live a productive and accomplished life. If you're like me, though, sometimes having goals seems overwhelming. Just as I use to do, instead of setting goals and working towards them, you may opt for not setting them at all because it's easier and more comfortable. There is nothing to fall short of, so there is nothing to fear, right? No! This shithole mindset will leave you wallowing in the ocean of all the other conformists, never to experience the magic of how it feels to build and sustain your own freedom empire! The only thing you need to set goals and achieve them is motivation and action. You already have the motivation, or you wouldn't be reading this. You have already set your goals, so you are on a rampage already! So how do you implement the action EVERY DAY to bring these goals to life?

While on my journey, I started devouring books, courses, podcasts, and blogs on setting goals and achieving them. As soon as I finished absorbing one of the practices, I fist pumped and raged like crazy thinking it was the key to the rest of my life. I dedicated myself to the system, planned it out, put it in place, and then started using it like a freight train! Except, my freight train would derail as soon as I picked up the next book or information product that showed me a different way to do it. I would go looney again and set up the new system, ready to rage! I tried daily time blocking, weekly streaks, 21-day plans, 30-day plans, 100-day plans, annual plans (yuck). The process ran in circles for about six months before I realized I was going about it ALL WRONG.

It didn't matter what system I used. What mattered was focusing on my goals and working towards them every day as a priority over all other things that "needed" to be done. It seems so obvious, but it's something we all overlook. What we do in the short term, in the moment, is the seed for everything we will manifest in the future. The more action we take in the short term to work on something, the faster it comes to life. If I work on my Spanish for 20 minutes each month, then it will most likely take decades before I know even the basics of Spanish. If I work on my Spanish for 20 minutes each day over a 100 day period, I'll be speaking basic Spanish within 100 days! Twenty minutes per day over 100 Days is 33.33 hours of Spanish - the near equivalent of a semester course.

Creating a daily habit to work on what is MOST IMPORTANT over all other to-do list items is the key to bringing your vision to reality. I've had the pleasure of interviewing multiple International, NY-Times, and Amazon best-selling authors, including the lovely Honoree Corder who has sold over 500,000 copies of her books including Vision to Reality, Prosperity for Writers, and You Must Write a Book. If you ask Honoree about the key to her writing success, she will tell you that it all starts with simply writing EVERY DAY, over anything else. She lets nothing stand in the way of her daily writing habit. Thus nothing can stop her from achieving her goals (like selling 500,000 books ☺)

When my goal was to create a network of successful entrepreneurs and share their skill sets with others, I geared my two daily freedom actions toward creating new connections with potential guests, editing podcasts, and conducting interviews.

When my goal was to pay off my personal debt, I geared my two freedom actions each day toward financial restructuring, like eliminating unnecessary bills and aggressively saving.

When my goal was to build an ecommerce business and scale it to $40,000 in monthly recurring revenue (I didn't fancy in my wildest dreams that I would hit 6 figures per month in revenue when I started), I geared my actions toward sourcing more products, hiring assistants, and meeting daily goals for purchasing and sales.

When you picked up this journal, you planted the seeds for manifesting your success. Whatever you are working toward (your freedom buds), literally picture them as the bud of a flower. To get from the seeds to the buds, you must supply the energy needed to grow the stems! Your daily freedom actions will grow into beautiful buds if you supply them with your essential energy. If you use your essential energy on other things like dicking around on Facebook or picking your butt and watching reality television, there won't be any energy for your buds to bloom.

Before I became inspired with the idea for this journal, I wrote my two actions on a single blank note card every morning and carried it with me throughout the day as a reminder to use my energy on these actions before all other things. I log my actions in my journal today, but I still jot them down on a notecard and keep them in my pocket as a reminder. There is never any harm in double checking yourself!

Set your daily freedom actions in direct relation to the freedom buds you are working toward, and use your best energy to complete these actions before all other things. If you can do this every day, you will blow the top off your campaign for happiness, freedom, and success.

Giving and Being Minimal

What will I give and/or minimize today?

Minimizing
When I was most unhappy, in debt, and confused about the direction of my life, I had a four-bedroom house full of endless furniture, clothes, junk drawers, and an infinite selection of "things" to take care of.

Because I had all these things distracting me, I never felt unproductive because I was always doing something to upkeep and manage my stuff. But, there is a huge difference between being productive in ways that matter to contribute to your freedom and happiness versus being productive in ways that provide zero value or purpose in life. Running around like a maniac all day to get the supplies I needed to fix, upgrade, and clean the junk in my house, and then actually fixing, updating, and cleaning the junk, was how I spent my weekends. At the end of the weekend, I felt good because the 1,200 items in my house were in place, I'd cleaned the fish tanks, and I could finally relax and have a beer before returning to work on Monday morning.

It wasn't until I discovered a little secret that I was able to start my campaign to remove distractions, eliminate debt, create clarity, and eventually create the life that I once thought was impossible.

You don't own your things. Your things own you! You must send them packing if you want to manifest freedom!

The habit of minimizing your distractions (social media, email, family, friends, material belongings, cell phones, etc.) will fuel your focus and eliminate obstacles that cause anxiety, stress, worry and restriction.

During conversations with the creative entrepreneurs from my podcast, I quickly realized that most of them were minimalists.

- Digital Nomad and Adventurepreneur Jason Berwick lives out of two suitcases and has a rule that all his belongings must fit in his car so that he can always hit the road for a new adventure.
- Bestselling author of over 21 books, Honoree Corder, moved out of her dream house and into an apartment with her daughter to find clarity, despite being ultra successful.
- Author and Life Coach Melissa Krivachek was sitting on the floor of an empty room during our interview!
- Dave Lent, director of the famous PBS documentary, Life Without: A Documentary from Inside San Quentin Prison, preferred minimalism because it forced more interaction with objects and value outside of the home!

These are just a few examples of the minimalists who happened to be successful entrepreneurs that came on my show.

When you have less stuff, you have fewer distractions. When you have fewer distractions, you awaken your awareness. When you are more aware, you pay attention to the areas of life that matter the most, like forming stronger relationships and engaging in higher levels of creativity.

As you form stronger relationships and engage in higher levels of creativity, and even combine the two, you continuously open up new doors that lead directly to clarity, purpose, and meaning in life.

When you live your life with a clear intent, you will discover that the pursuit of happiness you dream of is not only possible, it's absolute.

Clear intent allows direct focus on creating purpose, value, and meaning in life, which is the only way to create true happiness and freedom. Other perks stem from minimalism, too, like eliminating the emotional and physical COST of all these things. These costs are much greater than you think.

When you have things, there are costs involved with taking care of, accessorizing, upgrading, updating, charging, storing, maintaining, worrying about, thinking about, dusting, cleaning, protecting and even replacing ALL THINGS. And, you are spending your time, money, energy, and brainpower to make sure all of the above are taken care of, leaving little time, money, energy and brainpower for carving out and working toward the magnificent future you desire and deserve!

When I first started my campaign to become minimal, I followed the lead of The Minimalists (Joshua Fields Millburn and Ryan Nicodemus.) These guys hit home with me because they were from Dayton, OH, near me in Lexington KY, and both had left their corporate careers and created their dream life, all through discovering and teaching the act of minimalism. I highly suggest following them at TheMinimalists.com. They have amazing posts about the freedom of being minimal and how to deal with things like keepsakes, collections, photo albums and more. They also recently put out a documentary on Netflix called Minimalism: A Documentary About the Important Things, which is incredible.

To get started on your journey to become more minimal, here are some games that Josh and Ryan teach for beginners:

30 days of Minimalism Game - You can do this alone, or partner up with a friend (more fun and more accountability). Each day, for 30 days, you will get rid of the number of items for whatever day you are on. For example: On day one, you get rid of 1 thing. On day two, you get rid of 2 more things. On day 30, you get rid of 30 more things! Yes, this may seem like it's too much, but you will discover you have WAY MORE stuff than you ever imagined that is of little value to you. When I did this campaign, I put a Post-It note on each day's worth of items and took a picture. I kept all my pictures as motivation for the transformation I was undertaking. The first few days may seem easy, but then you will face harder decisions to get rid of things you're attached to. This fear is totally normal, but I promise you, once you get rid of those 'hard' items, you will forget you ever had them. When I reached day 30, I was so addicted to the feeling of freedom that I kept going. I made it all the way to day 58 before eliminating all my stuff! It was the best feeling I had experienced in over a decade of my life. The seed of freedom!

Packing Party Game - Ryan Nicodemus used this process when starting his journey. It is simple: You pack your house up like you are moving. Everything. Over the next two weeks, anything you 'need' you can pull out of the box and keep. These are the valuable items in your life that you are actually using. This doesn't mean unpack full boxes of junk and put them back on your shelf. If you run into a situation where you actually need something, then it's safe to remove and keep. These will be things like your favorite clothes, your favorite dishes, bath and toiletry items, and a few tools. After the two weeks is up, sell, donate, or trash the rest of the items. You won't miss them!

I'm fully aware that these are two very extreme approaches, and they aren't for everyone! If you really love your possessions and they don't get in the way of your quest for freedom and happiness, I still urge you to try and de-clutter other areas of your life, like email, social media, relationships, and more!

As this practice becomes a habit, continue to push yourself to sustain a minimal and distraction-free life. You may discover you are starting to collect a bunch of junk again (it happens), and there is a great method for controlling this also! Whenever you bring something new of value into your life, hold yourself accountable to get rid of something else that is no longer valuable. If you can do this, you will be a champion of minimalism!

Whenever questioning an item's worth, simply ask yourself, "Does this contribute absolute value to my life?" and if the answer is yes, keep it. If not, donate it, trash it, sell it, or send it off to someone who will find absolute value in it as a gift (which brings me to the next topic).

Me during my minimalist challenge

Giving

As media and marketing flood our brains with the idea that success is defined by how much we earn, many of us rate our happiness based on the materialistic belongings and monetary value we stack up. As soon as we receive something, we immediately start craving even more! We are rarely content with what we already have. Having a desire for more is a great characteristic when it comes to creativity and developing the self, but a terrible characteristic when it comes to stacking our cheese and junk piles.

I was the prototype for the American dream. I had tunnel vision on increasing my income at work and buying bigger and better things for the rest of my life, but I was miserable. Even though I had more money and stuff than ever, my happiness progressively declined. I wanted to feel that warm fuzzy feeling that we all use to get as children when we were excited, but it seemed impossible to track down.

I'm not arguing that receiving gifts, raises, and nicer things doesn't make us feel good momentarily, but it doesn't create and sustain happiness long-term.

If receiving more of everything isn't the answer to happiness, then what is?

Giving!

When you give something to another person, whether material or in service, a physiological response happens within you. That warm fuzzy feeling comes back, and it lets you make sexy time with your happiness muscle. Your brain releases pleasure endorphins, including oxytocin, which is also released during sex and lowers your stress. Oxytocin also makes you feel more connected to others, which is why people often pay forward random acts of kindness. I bet there has been a time in your life when someone did something nice for you or even gave you a gift without an occasion. I bet you paid it forward to someone else when you had the chance! It's a domino cycle of warm fuzzy feelings that increases the bond of the world!

While I was playing the 30 days of minimalism game, I became annoyed trying to sell stuff to looney bin sideshow freaks on Craigslist who bartered the price down to the floor and then didn't even show up. So I started looking into other options such as donating, gifting, and trashing. I had recently interviewed the big-hearted Valerie Groth, founder of the Ryan Banks Academy (if you want to give your first charity contribution,

I suggest checking out the RBA), on my podcast and she introduced me to the book 29 Gifts by Cami Walker. Woah! What a powerful book! The principle of the book became the foundation for why I started giving gifts and journaling about them, and why the practice became a part of this journal.

The rules of the 29 Gifts book are very simple. Give one gift away each day for 29 days, and see how it changes your life. Each gift must be thoughtful, and the more scarce to your life, the better! Since I was removing items from my life of zero value to me, the book opened my eyes to the possibility that there may be serious value in these items for others!

As I started giving away gifts and good deeds, I always made sure they would be of value to whoever was receiving them. It felt awesome and meaningful, but it wasn't until a few days in that I really discovered the true high of giving and providing value to others.

I had just listed my basement refrigerator on Craigslist and had an overwhelming response of maniacs blow up my email with the typical Craigslist donkey turd bartering system. I found the only response that seemed somewhat normal and replied saying the refrigerator was still available. They came later in the day to get it as promised (which is unusual on Craigslist) and pulled up in a red truck.

They had traveled over an hour from Cincinnati, OH to Lexington, KY to purchase the fridge. They looked at the unit and happily exchanged their money for it. I helped them load it into the back of the truck. They forgot to bring straps to tie it down, so I gave them a few extra that I had laying around the house. I could have easily used that as my gift for the day since the straps were providing value to help them transport the refrigerator back to Cincinnati, but as I walked inside and waved goodbye, I had an overwhelming feeling that I needed to give them their money back.

Without hesitation, I honored my feeling, running back out to their truck to give them the money. Their faces bore looks of confusion, as though they thought I wanted the fridge back. I simply said "A gift from me to you. Please pass on the good deed to someone else when the chance arises."

Huge smiles broke out on their faces now. They questioned my sanity, and then told me they had raised the money to buy the fridge for a family in need that didn't have one! I was blown away! They were already giving a gift themselves for a GREAT value, and in return, the universe was giving them one back. I was so happy to be on the helping end, and the feeling I had watching them drive away is something for which I will always keep striving!

A few days later I found a charity that collected musical instruments for children who couldn't afford them. We had an older cello laying around, and my fiancée Lindsay wanted to donate it to the cause. I grabbed a few other old guitars and took them down to the charity. As soon as the lady came out to the car to look at what we had, she FREAKED OUT over that cello! I didn't understand why she was so excited over this old cello, but she explained that they had a little girl who had been learning the cello. They didn't have any extras for her to take home and practice. Now she would have her own cello to take home! Again, the warm fuzzy feeling took over my body. It's a high that feels more divine than any other feeling in the world.

The universe will give you what you put into it, so don't think so much about what you are losing. Think about what you will gain.

I have gained peace and serenity. I have gained a constant warm fuzzy feeling that I lost for 15 years of my life. I have gained an intimate connectedness with others doing special things in the world.

To this day, this practice is the gateway to my connection and peace with others. No feeling matches the one I receive when I give with purpose.

Here are some ideas for giving gifts and good deeds:

- Go through the items you are purging during your minimalist campaign and see if any of them would be of value to anyone you know
- Invite the neighbors over for a casual meal
- Buy a coffee for the person behind you at a coffee shop
- Write a thank you note to someone who has been of great influence or importance to your life
- Call your family and friends and tell them you love them
- Volunteer at the local retirement homes and homeless shelters
- Pick up trash on the side of the road if you stumble upon it
- Offer your seat to someone else on the crowded bus or subway
- Help someone who is less fortunate or in need of food, clothing, or shelter
- Buy me a taser so I can protect myself from Craigslist maniacs
- Make contributions to charities of your choice (doing this anonymously is even better!). Some of my favorites are Jacaranda Health (www.jacarandahealth.org), The Ryan Banks Academy (www.ryanbanksacademy.org), Positive Legacy (www.positivelegacy.com), and Pencils of Promise (www.pencilsofpromise.org)
- Buy someone a gym membership
- Take a piece of dessert to someone at work
- Give someone a free corndog (advice from Kid President)
- Pick some fresh flowers for your significant other (dudes like flowers, too!)
- Send an email to an old teacher or friend
- Plant some trees
- Mow your neighbor's lawn
- Forgive someone you may be holding a grudge against
- Offer to babysit for someone, so they can go out and enjoy themselves for a night
- Give someone an album that you enjoy
- Take someone on vacation with you (If you have travel points, you could use those!)
- If you have a garden, share the fruits and vegetables with others
- Give a copy of this sweet ass journal to someone else!

Do your best to give gifts and provide good deeds as you blast your way through 100 days of defining your happiness muscle. Being minimal and giving more are habits that will help pump up your happiness muscle for the rest of your life, allowing you to discover true bliss and freedom. Try to do at least one or the other every day, and both as often as possible! Be a catalyst for the domino effect of happiness! Infinite warm fuzzy feelings await you!

EVENING SECTIONS
GUIDE

Winning

My wins for the day are...

When I was in the dark trenches, desperate to find some guidance from a different point of view outside of my body, I hired a life coach, even though I couldn't afford it. Jacqueline du Plessis had the life I desired - roaming around the world and helping others discover freedom. Jacqueline is optimistic because she understands the power of the mind. She is successful because she refuses to accept anything else. I learned some of the greatest habits of my life from Jacqueline, and I am living proof that they work.

If we think positively, our lives become positive. If we think negatively, we will get ass pounded by negativity gremlins until we change our mindsets. Jacqueline taught me that no matter how bad I think life is getting, it's all a means to opportunity. Everything we encounter, no matter how brutal it may seem, is an opportunity to heal and come back as a bigger, stronger ax wielding warrior for freedom. Instead of complaining about my job, I should be positive that I have a job which is allowing me to support my life while I venture out to create my dream life on the side. Instead of focusing on all the things that aren't going the way I want, I should focus on all the things that are going the way I want.

Jacqueline taught me that problems are our homies, our peeps, and our friends. We should be grateful that there will always be problems because this means there will always be opportunities to solve these problems creatively. Without these opportunities, we would have nothing to develop toward. Opportunities open the door to unlimited possibility of freedom, happiness, and purpose. Freedom is for those who love to solve problems, and pacifiers and poopy-pants are for those who don't.

I asked Jacqueline how to train myself to focus on the positives, and she simply asked me to write down my WINS for the day before I went to sleep. Then, once a week, we would go over them together.

"That's it?"
"Yeah, that's it."

So I wrote down my wins every night, as awkward as it felt. At first, it was difficult. I couldn't think of anything I considered a WIN because the term seems so powerful. I was waiting for the home runs and overlooking the plays.

After our first review, my lists were short and pathetic. I even included some of the bad things I did because I couldn't think of anything else. She quickly steered me in the right direction!

"Write down EVERYTHING you do throughout the day, except the things you aren't proud of. We do NOT want to focus on the negatives, remember? It will only attract more negativity! Write down anything and everything you do, as long as you are doing something that is moving you forward!"

From that point on, I was writing wins like a lunatic. If I brushed my teeth, I put it on the list. If I walked my dogs, I put it on the list. If I sent an email, I put it on the list! Soon, seeing how many things I was actually doing in a day blew my mind. Although many of them only required the skillset of a third grader, it carved my happiness muscle around the idea that I am capable. I started looking at life like a videogame, and for every level I blasted through during the day, I earned points. Nasty gremlin bosses popped in and tried to destroy me as I inched closer to completing each level, but I curb stomped those weenies and prevailed.

As I reflected on my wins at the end of each day, I didn't have to give my streaks, energy, or fire-powers back before starting the next day. It motivated me to keep going and grinding. To keep slaying gremlins and shaping the happiness muscle around my accomplishments.

When you do this practice, you'll start paying attention to the beauty in all things, big and small. You will start to appreciate the 10 minutes alone you had with your significant other in the midst of a hyperactive day. You will start to cherish parts of life that we rarely even think about, like our ability to wake up every morning, see the love around us, and use our magical hands and brains to bring creations into the world. You will start to understand that life is full of wins in each moment that we experience. I am winning because I am writing this right now. You are winning because you are reading it. We are winning because we are alive, and breathing, and experiencing this world with all of our senses. Everything is in its right place.

So before you lay your pretty little head down on your pillow, haystack, or giant furry pup at night to go to sleep (sorry cat people), start your PM practice by writing down your WINS for the day. Don't just write the big things. Write anything and everything you do that contributes to your moving forward! Waking up is a gift! Eating your meals is a gift! Returning safely from work is a gift! As you continue this practice, you'll start to notice something incredible: Your wins will get bigger and more powerful. You will build a massive awareness of all that you accomplish, which will become a huge motivator to keep dominating.

Here are a few things I wrote down on my wins list from 1/3/2015:

- Woke up breathing in my bed and not face-down pants-down in the bushes.
- Did my miracle morning practice.
- Walked outside and looked at the stars before the sun came up.
- Came in under budget on my 'career' expense report. Should get bonus.
- Ran my first 4 miles of the year.
- Bid a new website project for $3,000.

- Fixed the motor inducer in our heater.
- Mapped out a plan for a healthy streak!
- Created a new bills and budget spreadsheet to help manage cash flow and eliminate debt
- Started a fun minimalist game with Lindsay to get rid of all the junk we own that isn't valuable to us.
- Spent awesome quality time with the family.
- Created a very rough sketch of how a podcast flows for podcasting business idea.
- Sent an email to an SEO guy in Utah about creating an affiliate relationship.
- Signed up for an Amazon seller account
- Moved my fish tank

This was before I was writing EVERYTHING, but I wanted to share it because it was an ambitious time - the beginning of the year. I was bidding website projects for my old business (which ultimately failed), doing sketches of a podcasting business that I would eventually start and fail. It was the first day I signed up for my Amazon account (which is the base of my business now), and it's also the day I started my minimalist challenge. It gives me chills to think about how much has changed in just two years.

Now it's your turn to create the magic. Each day is a mini battle in your war against resistance gremlins, and each win you have throughout the day is a blow to the heart of those slimy little bastards. Every night, dedicate a few minutes to writing down all your wins! Start the streak. Keep winning the battles. Defeat the gremlins. Win the war for your freedom.

Abundance List

I have an abundance of...

Just as we celebrate our wins to reflect on our momentum and juice up our motivation, it is equally important to celebrate our abundance.

I have already stressed the importance of eliminating mental and physical distractions and practicing gratitude for all that you have. It is equally important to express gratitude for the valuable mental and physical compadres we have fighting with us, sustaining us while we work toward more meaningful and powerful experiences. The things that survive your minimalist shedding are items of value that contribute to your mission in some way or another. All the people around you who support your journey contribute to your mission! Every educational and exploratory experience in your life has carved your miraculous array of skillsets that you now use as your ammunition to destroy resistance gremlins and dominate your freedom empire. We can identify and eliminate the toxic things in life that keep us from moving at champion speed toward our dreams, but we can also pause to appreciate all of the value surrounding us in support of our quest.

People, materials, skillsets, experiences, and even the basic elements of life - everything supporting your journey - is your abundance. You must pause and reflect often on just how big and beautiful your arsenal of abundance is so you can defeat the gremlins that make you feel like you don't have enough.

Anti-abundance gremlins are the little bastards whispering atrocious things into your thoughts, like "If I just had a little more time, I could do these awesome things." Or, "If I just had a little more money, I could afford to do these awesome things." Or, "If I just had someone to help me, I'd be able to do these awesome things." They want you to focus on what you don't have. They want you to feel like you are limited in your abilities. They throw new-years caliber black-out parties with oodles of narcotics and disco balls every time you fail to recognize gratitude for what you already have. Remember, focusing on the negative will only breed more negativity into your life. Following the lead of the anti-abundance gremlins will lead you down a dead-end alley where you will get mugged (and possibly molested) by limitation.

You MUST understand that you have anything and everything you need, right now, to develop into a happier, more valuable, sweet ass version of you!

We are all human. We all experience peaks in our emotions on both ends of the spectrum, but using the evening to reflect on the amazing abundance we DO have will keep the dickhead doubter gremlins locked in their slime layer and allow us to focus on the positives while we blast our rockets to Planet Happiness.

In this section, write down anything and everything in your life that supports you in your journey. These are the seeds of your abundance, and they will only sprout and grow into trees without limitation if you recognize their existence and support them! You can even take it a step further and write out how the abundance of 'X' impacts your life. There is no wrong way to do this, so be as simple or detailed as you wish!

Some examples to get that sexy mind flowing:

- I have an abundance of energy which allows me to create
- I have an abundance of sunlight which allows me to re-energize
- I have an abundance of fresh air which allows me to breathe
- I have an abundance of family members who support me
- I have an abundance of transportation available to me
- I have an abundance of free resources online to help me learn anything imaginable
- I have an abundance of time to relax and enjoy the company of my loved ones
- I have an abundance of water available to me for drinking, hygiene, and washing my abundance of clothes
- I have an abundance of undies
- I have an abundance of rice and beans
- I have an abundance of money because I am alive and able to care for myself
- I have an abundance of honey and tea to help kickstart the day
- I have an abundance of Arnold Schwarzenegger merchandise
- I have an abundance of trails, mountains, lakes, trees, and parks around me where I can bond with the great outdoors
- I have an abundance of skills which allow me to support myself and my family

- I have an abundance of awesome people who will soon come into my life
- I have an abundance of Gold Bond for when I get a bad case of the swamp-ass
- I have an abundance of gifts I can give others to brighten up their day
- I have an abundance of outlets to charge my electronics
- I have an abundance of weapons to mutilate resistance gremlins
- I have an abundance of resting places to rejuvenate the mind and body
- I have an abundance of dreams which I will manifest
- I have an abundance of happiness
- I have an abundance of freedom
- I have an abundance of creativity
- I have an abundance of opportunity ahead of me

As you practice your abundance list, you will quickly shape your awareness around all the positive support in your life. If you ever find yourself as the host for a gremlin blackout disco-ball bonanza (those Jabronis never stop trying to party), remember to shift your focus from what you don't have to what you DO! When you think positive, you will breed more positive. Make sexy-time with your abundance and pop out some positive juju babies. You are in a position to be as happy and free as you decide to be, and your abundance will grow alongside of you.

Tomorrow's Freedom Actions

What are the two most valuable freedom actions I will take tomorrow to progress towards my vision, goals, and dream life?

Just as you set your awesome freedom actions for the day, it's just as important to plan out the following day's actions at night. By setting your intentions to dominate the following day before you go to sleep at night, you prepare your brain for success the next day.

Nighttime is the perfect time to reflect on your progress for the day, allowing you to easily focus in on the next important step in your journey to grow and bloom your sweet ass freedom buds. You won't lay in bed at night thinking about all the possible things you may have to do tomorrow. Instead, you will accomplish a state of relaxation, and your body and mind will get the rest they need to become your war tanks of efficiency and effectiveness in your daily battles against the gremlins. You will subconsciously encourage yourself to wake up earlier because you have a purpose for the day. Because you have a purpose, you will be in a much stronger position to judo-chop the procrastination gremlins in the throat before they can even haunt your thoughts.

Every day we are faced with multiple decisions and unique problem-solving scenarios, so setting our intentions the night before will help reserve the will power we need for other parts of life throughout the day.

Yes, it may seem redundant writing your freedom actions the night before AND the morning of your rampage, but think of it as an opportunity for extra preparation. When you are more prepared, you are more likely to feel motivated and confident, and you will position yourself for success.

Remember to focus on the two most important actions for the following day (as discussed in the AM freedom actions section) and to attack the scariest and hairiest first! When you accomplish the action you most fear before anything else, the rest of the day is like busting into the secret levels in a video game. Everything becomes a bonus round!

Nightly Affirmations. I am...

"I think about how great it all will be. Then, it happens to me."

How we got here

Because you are reading this, you're probably already thinking about ways to become a better version of you. We've already talked about how positive thoughts will breed more positivity in your life, and negative thoughts will breed more negativity in your life. Being a glass half full person will do wonders on its own, but what if I told you that you could become anyone and experience anything you want if you only think about them in the present tense?

Most of us grow up unaware of this power, and we tend to think about our current situations and our futures based off of the ideas of how society thinks we should be. And, before we know it, we are feeling unhappy, lost, and out of touch with our dreams and our visions.

When I worked in the concrete industry, I often asked myself, "How in the hell did I get here?" I sat on job sites in the mountains of Eastern Kentucky at 4:00 a.m. to test the air content of concrete mixtures (don't ask), always feeling sorry for myself as if I had no control over my position. I honestly believed that I didn't have a choice and that it was just the direction my life took because it was the best option for creating a stable job and income to support myself. But I had become this person because I allowed myself to think that this person was the solution to my health and stability. Since the school I went to didn't have a geology major - my real interest as a kid - I signed up for the next best thing: creating artificial rocks (AKA concrete). From that point on, I viewed the industry as an opportunity to get a great job and salary out of college, and to set myself up for a long career.

In my head, I decided my future would involve making a great income climbing the corporate ladder, and that is exactly how the next ten years of my life went. I climbed ladders, made money, and rounded out my late twenties as a 'successful' conformist of the American Dream. I even lived in a nice house with a bunch of really nice things, despite the growing pile of loans and debt which I thought were necessary to get on top. I would never have admitted it back then, but I was only in that position because I thought about that position. I was a product of how I imagined my life. I had dreams, sure, but when I came "back to reality" like society teaches, I always ended up accepting my situation. Because of this, I trod the path to an unfulfilling career in an industry that didn't interest me. I affirmed a life without true happiness and freedom. What a big silly goose I was back then.

You may feel like you are in a similar situation, wherever you may be in life. But you don't have to be! You don't have to climb the corporate ladder. There is certainly nothing wrong with making an 'honest' living and paying your bills, but if you feel empty or unhappy because of it, maybe it's time for a change! Look through the ladder and visualize the world of opportunity on the other side!

The only thing you MUST do to become the person you dream of is to think about becoming that person, and then make a commitment to move in that direction. If you truly believe the transformation you desire will come true, and you commit your freedom actions to work in unison with your beliefs, you can manifest the life of your dreams.

I am not implying that if you think of what you want, it will just magically appear without you doing anything. You must commit. Traditional affirmation practices may lead you to believe that you can just sit in your room and repeat "I am a skinny and fit millionaire" and it will come true. It will NEVER come true if you sit on your couch and eat buckets of fried chicken without making any commitment to bring it to life, I don't care how many times you repeat it per day. You cannot bring an affirmation to life unless you are committed to it with your mind and actions.

"We become what we think about." - Earl Nightingale

If you ask the universe for water, it will quench your thirst. If you support your vision with all your energy, your vision will come to pass. Whatever you are reaching for, in return, is reaching for you! You are the sculptor of your own life.

When Jacqueline du Plessis gifted me the audiobook version of Earl Nightingale's The Strangest Secret, my life changed forever. Before you continue this journal, please take a moment to listen to this 30-minute speech that will change your life. You can listen and gain access to other free resources from this journal by visiting **www.sweetassjournal. com/bonus**

Don't let the "I'll get around to it later" gremlins eat your soul and prevent you from listening to this. Either listen right now or write down a reminder to do it later. It's the most important gift you could give yourself. If you don't, you might as well poop your pants and get your pacifier back out! :)

Earl argues that we become what we think about. The thoughts we have about our lives directly determine the outcome of our lives. Each one of us is the sum total of our thoughts, and by thinking that we are great, we will become great.

This is not a new concept. Napoleon Hill's Think and Grow Rich expanded upon it, and so have other mass publications. I'd have to search hard to find anyone in the 100+ creative entrepreneurs I interviewed who didn't affirm their future to transform into the person they are today. In one conversation with Bri Seeley, founder of The Inspirational Woman Project, she elaborated on a morning routine in which she and few accountability friends had phone conversations where they addressed their future lives in the present tense.

They had conversations as their future selves, talking about how awesome their lives were and all the incredible things they were involved in (even though they weren't a reality yet). By doing this, they planted the seeds for their visions to manifest. (As you sow, so shall you reap.) Philosophers, religious leaders, and successful people since the history of documented literature have used the power of visualization to manifest desired outcomes in life.

Now it's your turn.

What do you want in life?

Take a moment right now to think about what you truly want in life.

- What do you want to accomplish in your short time on this beautiful planet?
- What do you want to accomplish in this moment? In your love life? In your career?
- Are there areas in your life that you want to improve, like your relationships, your health, or financial status?
- Do you have emotional pain points that need healing?
- Where do you want to live and travel?
- What have you always wanted to do more than anything in the world?
- Are there any new skillsets that you want to learn?
- What would make your experience on Earth more meaningful?
- What internal areas do you want to develop the most, such as self-image, confidence, honesty, bravery, respect?
- How many gremlins do you want to body-slam today?

How do the answers to these questions relate to the freedom buds that you set at the beginning of this journal? Whatever it is you want, you can and will have it if you set an intention and think about it every day. By thinking about it, you will prime your brain to influence your behavior and decisions in favor of your visions, and you will become what you think about.

To create your nightly affirmations, write your visions and desires in the present tense, then repeat them out loud three times each. If you want to get a little fancier, add on an action to the end of the affirmation that supports how you will achieve the affirmation. This extra step will program both your conscious and subconscious mind to focus on the results you desire.

When I first started writing my affirmations, I made zero money outside my job, I was NOT location independent, and I had a walk-in closet full of internal emotional issues I was running from. But I answered all of the questions above, and I started writing my affirmations every night and repeating them out loud.

Here are some examples of what I wrote:

- I make $100 extra per month on a side business.
- I am confident and excited when I speak in public because I have nothing to fear.
- I save $200 a week by being aware of my spending, and I use it to pay off my debt.
- I am so happy and grateful for each moment of my life.
- I am focused on my vision, and nothing can stop me.
- I wake up at 5:00 every morning to meditate, read, write, and practice my guitar.
- I am happy, healthy and full of clarity because I decide to be.

About a year later, all of the things above had manifested (except the public speaking fear which I still battle today), and I was writing affirmations like this:

- I am selling $85,000/month in my Amazon business because I focus on scalability and growth.
- I am location independent because I love to travel and I keep physical distractions out of my life.
- I write 1,000 words per day to support my future as an author.
- I am healthy and pain-free because I work out and stretch every day.

All of these have now manifested, and I'm currently writing affirmations such as:

- I sell $150k/month on Amazon because I focus on scalability and growth.
- I create and sell my own products that help people discover happiness.
- I am a bestselling author because I teach from my heart.
- I speak intermediate Spanish.
- I am hiking the entire Appalachian Trail while my business continues to generate revenue.

- My emotional fear is an illusion. I am a space ape made of stardust, flying through space on a giant rock at 67,000 MPH around a giant ball of fire.
- I travel the world and support great causes with my monetary abundance and services.
- With every choice, I am one decision away from improving my quest for being the best version of me possible.
- I am an ax-wielding warrior, and nothing can stand in the way of my life of happiness and freedom.
- Everything I desire is on its way to me at warp speed.
- Every problem I have breeds the opportunity for a solution. I live for creating these solutions and sharing them with others!

One of my current passion projects is a deck of awesome motivation and affirmation cards for creatives and entrepreneurs. You can check out the cards and all of my current and upcoming projects at **heatharmstrong.com/projects**

It's your turn! In this section, write out your affirmations and repeat them out loud. Start with some simple affirmations, and you will naturally work your way into the miracle stages. When you read them, visualize them playing like a movie in your head at the same time. If you can do this simple practice, you will juice your brain to focus on becoming this new sweet ass version of you, and your decisions and behavior will start to bring your visions to the present tense. Make the commitment to link your freedom actions to your affirmations, and you will become what you think about.

I'll catch you on the flip side!

Silent Awareness

2+ Minutes of Meditation and Deep Breathing

The most important habit that I've developed over my obsessive rampage to form life-changing habits is meditation. Honestly, nothing else even comes close. By practicing meditation, I have been able to keep my mind at its highest power, allowing me to form other habits, eliminate stress gremlins on demand, and focus on what matters most in each moment.

I'm not proud to admit I was once the guy that laughed at people who meditated. Every time I thought about meditation, the hilarious scene of Jim Carrey meditating in the hut (the extended 'Alrighty Then' chant) from Ace Ventura: When Nature Calls flooded my mind with comedy. I thought it was ridiculous in every way possible. My mind constantly bounced around at the speed of light, and I was simply a passenger following it wherever it wanted to go. I'm totally proud to admit I couldn't have been more wrong about meditation. I trace every step of my success back to the first day I sat down to attempt a meditation. I heard a podcast interview with Kim Nicol, a lawyer in San Francisco who left her high-stress career (after her co-worker got hit and killed by a bus as she was walking into her office) to teach other lawyers how to manage stress and reclaim their lives via meditation, and I fell in love with her story. I reached out to her, and she helped me get started with a beginner meditation series that she created called "5 Mindful Minutes."

Eventually, I had her as one of the first interviewees on my podcast, and I've been an avid fan of her practice and work ever since. As my interviews kept rolling, I noticed almost every successful person I talked with also engaged in frequent meditation, and I realized this habit was a legit life changer. (Check out Kim Nicol's interview, as well as other great mindful teachers such as Erik Stenqvist, Jeena Cho, and Molly Knight Forde on *HeathArmstrong.com/interviews*).

After practicing for a few years now, the most important power meditation has blessed me with is the ability to observe my thoughts rather than react to them. Sure, I still chase my thoughts and fall victim to overwhelming stress and other emotions, but far less frequently than I use to. I am more aware of the commands my mind is giving me, and I can analyze the commands before reacting, which grants me a certain freedom and peacefulness I never experienced before. Meditation allows me to focus and develop areas of my life that are in alignment with my visions and dreams, most of which are practices in other sections of this journal.

I know the word meditation alone can seem daunting, but I once felt that way, too. If not for Kim's easy practice to get me started, I'm not sure I would have seen it all the way through. I assure you that if I hadn't, this journal wouldn't be in your hands today, and I'd probably still be on a construction jobsite at 3:00 a.m. in Kentucky somewhere.

If you already practice meditation, you are smiling because you know how awesome it is. If you don't, it is my HONOR to help guide you to your new super power. Nothing hard. Nothing fancy. Just a few moments each day or night to pay homage to your beautiful mind. I prefer the morning because meditation allows me to find clarity in my approach to this journal and the overall outlook of the day, but I know others who are much more into meditation at night. I also take moments to do brief meditations whenever I feel stressed or overwhelmed. There is no right or wrong time to meditate, so just do it when it feels right for you. Over time, you may discover the magic and develop into a meditation machine, living with the Monks in a Temple in the mountains of Thailand. You may even develop a sweet 'Alrighty Then' chant like Ace Ventura. But, for now, let's keep it short and sweet! You can adapt this to your own comfort level.

Actions for starting your daily practice of silent awareness:

- Find or create a quiet space where you feel comfortable and removed from distractions. (for a free guide on creating an awesome sacred space, visit *www.sweetassjournal.com/bonus*).
- Sit or lay down comfortably.
- Put on some soft mindful or classical music in the background, or simply tune into the noise of your surroundings and nature.
- Check out the Insight Meditation Timer app for Apple or Android for free guided meditations, music, a meditation timer, tracking your practice and more! Hunt me down and add me as a friend!
- Close your eyes.
- For just a few minutes, breathe in and out, focusing on each breath.

- When your mind starts to wander (it will), bring your attention back to your breath.
- A good trick is to count seconds as you breathe. Breathe in for 5 seconds, hold it for 5 seconds, breathe out for 5 seconds, hold it for 5 seconds, etc.)
- When you're ready, open your eyes and observe how you feel.

That's it!

Just a few minutes of silent awareness each day can lay a foundation for changing your entire approach to life. As you develop this habit, you can add to the length of your meditations or plug the practice in when you feel like your brain needs a reset. There are no limits.

When you fill out your reflection section at the end of the journal each day, note how many minutes you dedicated to your meditation practice and how you felt during and after the meditation. If you meditate in the morning, use the practice to help guide you in your approach to the other sections of the journal. If you meditate in the evening, allow it to serve as a reflection of the beautiful progress you made throughout the day!

Reflection

How awesome was today?

This section helps you reflect upon the awesomeness that you experienced throughout the day. It's a final check-in before you head to rest that pretty little face! Did you complete your freedom actions for the day? Did you give a gift and/or minimize? How did it feel? Did you find time to meditate? What did you observe?

Jot down a few simple notes about how awesome it all was, and get ready for another round of magic tomorrow!

As a human, you will naturally go through periods of streaks and droughts. It happens to all of us. The most important thing is to stay on track with creating the habit, and giving 110% effort whenever possible to maximize our awakening for freedom and happiness. Don't be hard on yourself, but be proud for what you do accomplish. Every day is a bonus round taking us a step closer to freedom!

PART 3:
THE JOURNAL

Time to Party and Never Give Up!

Because your freedom is worth it...

This journal is NOT intended to overwhelm you or cause you stress and anxiety. If it does, you are the exact type of person that should be using it! A few years ago, fearful and unhappy, I struggled to read books, journal, or even simply reflect on my life. I found it more comforting to ignore it than to create a habit to change for the better. Sadly, most of our lives go on forever this way, but this is a cold-hearted illusion dropped on us by those nasty resistance gremlins. They are shoving their slimy weenies in our eyes, clouding up our clarity and vision. We can chop those weenies off and defeat resistance with small, simple steps. Think of this journal as your secret weapon and feed it with energetic ammunition!

As I've created this process over the past year, at times, I did not even open the journal for weeks. Coincidently, those weeks were usually when I experienced high stress, doubt, lack of confidence, and zero creativity. When I'm on a roll and hitting three or four-week streaks, everything seems to fall into place, and my entire creative drive is blessed with magical results and opportunity. There is no doubt that this journal has become an anchor for the creation of my freedom empire, and as a result, an instigator of happiness.

Do this for your freedom, your happiness, and the person you deserve to become, no matter how big, small, briefly or extensively you write. Take a step forward every day with this journal and create a habit to develop your happiness muscle. Pump that thing up and keep it swollen! It will flow into so many other areas of your life, and you will see color where it's always been gray. As the world is constantly "looking" for happiness everywhere and failing to find it, you will be one of the few who creates it yourself.

As Dave Lent taught me,

> "When you follow your bliss, that thing that truly electrifies you, four things automatically happen: you put yourself in the path of good luck, you meet the people you want to know, doors open where there weren't doors before, and doors open for you that wouldn't open to anybody else."

I hope this journal helps you discover your superpowers and follow your bliss.

And, have a sweet ass time along the way!

EXAMPLE OF COMPLETED JOURNAL

DATE ..2.. / ..4.. / 20 ..17..

Every day is a bonus round. Slow down and enjoy something beautiful.
– Sohrab Mirmont

What makes me ☺ ?

MOUNTAINS! MY PUPS ☺
· ANOTHER DAY TO CREATE!
· WAKING UP IN MY WARM BED.
· THAT FEELING AFTER FINISHING
   A GOOD BOOK...
· THE THOUGHT OF SPRING

~ *TRAVEL* ~

What am I thankful for?

· MY FIANCÉE LINDSAY FOR
   SUPPORTING MY CRAZY DREAMS
· CALLER I.D. SO I CAN
   SCREEN CALLS FROM LUNATIC
   TELEMARKETERS.
· INCENSE
· THE QUIET HOURS IN THE
   MORNING WHEN EVERYONE
   ELSE IS ASLEEP
· MUSIC bc it KEEPS MY
   HEAD FROM EXPLODING

Sweet Ass Ideas for:
STRESS RELIEF

BASKETBALL , TRAIL RUN
MOUNTAIN BIKING, SAUNA
WORKING OUT, MEDITATION
PLAY GUITAR , CAMPING
TAKE PUPS TO THE PARK ,
FRISBEE GOLF , GO HAVE
A FEW CRAFT BEERS AT A
BREWERY – DE IN THE
MOMENT

What are the two **most valuable freedom actions** I will take today to progress toward my vision, goals, and dream life?

1. I will write
   1000 WORDS

2. I WILL WRITE OUT
   THE STEPS FOR ONE TASK
   I CAN DELEGATE TO
   AN ASSISTANT

What will I **give** and/or **minimize** today?

I'M GOING TO CLEAN OUT THE JUNK DRAWER
IN THE KITCHEN + CLEAR UP SOME SPACE ON MY
PHONE
= CALL MY FAMILY + TELL THEM I ♡ THEM.

My **wins** for the day are:

I woke up, showered, ate + incredible breakfast.

I DID MY MIRACLE MORNING + WROTE SOME GREAT THOUGHTS AFTER THE MEDITATION! LINDSAY MADE IT TO THE AIRPORT SAFELY. I CALLED MY FAMILY + TOLD THEM I LOVED THEM. I PAID BILLS. I SOLD 76 ITEMS ON AMAZON. I WROTE 1000 WORDS. I WATCHED A LIVE CONCERT ON YOUTUBE. I LEARNED HOW TO PLAY 'HURT' BY TRENT REZNOR ON GUITAR

I have an **abundance** of:

- GUIDED MEDITATIONS TO PLAY FROM.

- SOCKS TO KEEP MY GIANT FEET WARM

- Opportunities to create

- PLACES I CAN TAKE MINI VACATIONS TO

- HAIR TIES SO I CAN KEEP MY SWEET FLOWING HAIR BACK IN A PONY!

What are the two **most valuable freedom actions** I will take tomorrow to progress toward my vision, goals, and dream life?

1. I WILL FINISH 10 MORE AFFIRMATION CARDS FOR MY NEW PROJECT

2. I WILL REACH OUT TO A FEW DESIGNERS ABOUT DOING A PACKAGE DESIGN

Nightly Affirmations, I am...

- I AM SELLING MY OWN PRODUCTS ON AMAZON

- I AM HEALTHY AND PAIN FREE

Did I accomplish my two main freedom actions today? ☺ ☺ ☹

Did I give a gift and/or minimize? ☺ ☺ ☹

What was it and how did it feel? CLEANED OUT THE JUNK IN THE KITCHEN CALLED MY FAMILY - FELT GOOD.

I meditated for ...11... minutes today and I felt: Comfortable + light

You are 3 % done with developing your happiness muscle :)

DEVELOP YOUR HAPPINESS MUSCLE IN 100 DAYS

Please visit the following link for a **free audio version** of this guide, and to download a **free 100-day checklist** you can print and put on your wall to remind you to visit your journal and slay resistance gremlins!

www.sweetassjournal.com/bonus

DATE ……… / ……… / 20 ………

Every day is a bonus round. Slow down and enjoy something beautiful.
— Sohrab Mirmont

What makes me ☺ ?

What am I thankful for?

Sweet Ass Ideas for:

What are the two **most valuable freedom actions** I will take today to progress toward my vision, goals, and dream life?

1.

2.

What will I **give** and/or **minimize** today?

My **wins** for the day are:

I have an **abundance** of:

What are the two **most valuable freedom actions** I will take tomorrow to progress toward my vision, goals, and dream life?

1.

2.

Nightly Affirmations, I am...

Did I accomplish my two main freedom actions today?   ☺ ☺ ☹

Did I give a gift and/or minimize?   ☺ ☺ ☹

What was it and how did it feel? _____

I meditated for .... **minutes today and I felt:** _____

You are   **1%** done with developing your happiness muscle :)

DATE .... / .... / 20 ....

Break the rules, but first break the rulers.
– Sean Michael Daley (Slug)

What makes me ☺ ?

What am I thankful for?

Sweet Ass Ideas for:

What are the two **most valuable freedom actions** I will take today to progress toward my vision, goals, and dream life?

1.

2.

What will I **give** and/or **minimize** today?

My **wins** for the day are:

I have an **abundance** of:

What are the two **most valuable freedom actions** I will take tomorrow to progress toward my vision, goals, and dream life?

1.

2.

Nightly Affirmations, I am...

Did I accomplish my two main freedom actions today?   ☺ 😐 ☹

Did I give a gift and/or minimize?   ☺ 😐 ☹

What was it and how did it feel? _____

I meditated for .... minutes today and I felt: _____

You are   **2**% done with developing your happiness muscle :)

DATE .... / .... / 20 ....

Choose to face the fear of today, rather than the regret of forever.
– Jon Acuff

What makes me ☺ ?

What am I thankful for?

Sweet Ass Ideas for:

- -

What are the two **most valuable freedom actions** I will take today to progress toward my vision, goals, and dream life?

1.

2.

What will I **give** and/or **minimize** today?

My **wins** for the day are:

I have an **abundance** of:

What are the two **most valuable freedom actions** I will take tomorrow to progress toward my vision, goals, and dream life?

1.

2.

Nightly Affirmations, I am...

Did I accomplish my two main freedom actions today? ☺ ☻ ☹

Did I give a gift and/or minimize? ☺ ☻ ☹

What was it and how did it feel? _____

I meditated for .... **minutes today and I felt:** _____

You are   **3**% done with developing your happiness muscle :)

DATE .... / .... / 20 ....

Some poor, phoneless fool is probably sitting next to a waterfall somewhere totally unaware of how angry and scared he's suppose to be.
— Duncan Trussell

What makes me ☺ ?

What am I thankful for?

Sweet Ass Ideas for:

What are the two **most valuable freedom actions** I will take today to progress toward my vision, goals, and dream life?

1.

2.

What will I **give** and/or **minimize** today?

My **wins** for the day are:

I have an **abundance** of:

What are the two **most valuable freedom actions** I will take tomorrow to progress toward my vision, goals, and dream life?

1.

2.

Nightly Affirmations, I am...

Did I accomplish my two main freedom actions today? ☺ 😐 ☹

Did I give a gift and/or minimize? ☺ 😐 ☹

What was it and how did it feel? _____

I meditated for .... **minutes today and I felt:** _____

You are 4% done with developing your happiness muscle :)

DATE ………. / ………. / 20 ……….

Experiences are what set you on fire, not the new iPhone.
– Jason Berwick

What makes me ☺ ?

What am I thankful for?

Sweet Ass Ideas for:

- -

What are the two **most valuable freedom actions** I will take today to progress toward my vision, goals, and dream life?

1.

2.

What will I **give** and/or **minimize** today?

My **wins** for the day are:

I have an **abundance** of:

What are the two **most valuable freedom actions** I will take tomorrow to progress toward my vision, goals, and dream life?

1.

2.

Nightly Affirmations, I am...

Did I accomplish my two main freedom actions today? ☺ ☺ ☹

Did I give a gift and/or minimize? ☺ ☺ ☹

What was it and how did it feel? _____

I meditated for .... minutes today and I felt: _____

You are   **5**% done with developing your happiness muscle :)

DATE .... / .... / 20 ....

Do not dwell in the past,
do not dream of the future,
concentrate the mind on the present moment.
– Buddha

What makes me ☺ ?

What am I thankful for?

Sweet Ass Ideas for:

What are the two **most valuable freedom actions** I will take today to progress toward my vision, goals, and dream life?

1.

2.

What will I **give** and/or **minimize** today?

My **wins** for the day are:

I have an **abundance** of:

What are the two **most valuable freedom actions** I will take tomorrow to progress toward my vision, goals, and dream life?

1.

2.

Nightly Affirmations, I am...

Did I accomplish my two main freedom actions today? ☺ ☺ ☹

Did I give a gift and/or minimize? ☺ ☺ ☹

What was it and how did it feel? _____

I meditated for .... **minutes today and I felt:** _____

You are 6% done with developing your happiness muscle :)

DATE .... / .... / 20 ....

You can't see the label of the jar you are in.
– Valerie Groth

What makes me ☺ ?

What am I thankful for?

Sweet Ass Ideas for:

What are the two **most valuable freedom actions** I will take today to progress toward my vision, goals, and dream life?

1.

2.

What will I **give** and/or **minimize** today?

My **wins** for the day are:

I have an **abundance** of:

What are the two **most valuable freedom actions** I will take tomorrow to progress toward my vision, goals, and dream life?

1.

2.

Nightly Affirmations, I am...

Did I accomplish my two main freedom actions today? ☺ 😐 ☹

Did I give a gift and/or minimize? ☺ 😐 ☹

What was it and how did it feel? _____

I meditated for .... **minutes today and I felt:** _____

You are   7% done with developing your happiness muscle :)

DATE ………… / ………… / 20 ………

Believe you can and you're halfway there.
– Theodore Roosevelt

What makes me 😊 ?

What am I thankful for?

Sweet Ass Ideas for:

What are the two **most valuable freedom actions** I will take today to progress toward my vision, goals, and dream life?

1.

2.

What will I **give** and/or **minimize** today?

My **wins** for the day are:

I have an **abundance** of:

What are the two **most valuable freedom actions** I will take tomorrow to progress toward my vision, goals, and dream life?

1.

2.

Nightly Affirmations, I am...

Did I accomplish my two main freedom actions today? ☺ ☺ ☹

Did I give a gift and/or minimize? ☺ ☺ ☹

What was it and how did it feel? _____

I meditated for .... **minutes today and I felt:** _____

You are **8%** done with developing your happiness muscle :)

DATE ……… / ……… / 20 ………

There is nothing so wretched or foolish as to anticipate misfortunes.
What madness it is in your expecting evil before it arrives!
– Seneca

What makes me ☺ ?

What am I thankful for?

Sweet Ass Ideas for:

What are the two **most valuable freedom actions** I will take today to progress toward my vision, goals, and dream life?

1.

2.

What will I **give** and/or **minimize** today?

My **wins** for the day are:

I have an **abundance** of:

What are the two **most valuable freedom actions** I will take tomorrow to progress toward my vision, goals, and dream life?

1.

2.

Nightly Affirmations, I am...

Did I accomplish my two main freedom actions today? ☺ ☺ ☹

Did I give a gift and/or minimize? ☺ ☺ ☹

What was it and how did it feel? _____

I meditated for .... **minutes today and I felt:** _____

You are   **9** % done with developing your happiness muscle :)

DATE .... / .... / 20 ....

No matter how successful you are, you will still have the voice of doubt running around. You've got to shut her up, because she is not accurate.
– Honoree Corder

What makes me ☺ ?

What am I thankful for?

Sweet Ass Ideas for:

- -

What are the two **most valuable freedom actions** I will take today to progress toward my vision, goals, and dream life?

1.

2.

What will I **give** and/or **minimize** today?

My **wins** for the day are:

I have an **abundance** of:

What are the two **most valuable freedom actions** I will take tomorrow to progress toward my vision, goals, and dream life?

1.

2.

Nightly Affirmations, I am...

Did I accomplish my two main freedom actions today? ☺ ☺ ☹

Did I give a gift and/or minimize? ☺ ☺ ☹

What was it and how did it feel? _____

I meditated for .... **minutes today and I felt:** _____

You are   **10** % done with developing your happiness muscle :)

DATE .... / .... / 20 ....

Try to be a rainbow in someone's cloud.
– Maya Angelou

What makes me ☺ ?

What am I thankful for?

Sweet Ass Ideas for:

- -

What are the two **most valuable freedom actions** I will take today to progress toward my vision, goals, and dream life?

1.

2.

What will I **give** and/or **minimize** today?

My **wins** for the day are:

I have an **abundance** of:

What are the two **most valuable freedom actions** I will take tomorrow to progress toward my vision, goals, and dream life?

1.

2.

Nightly Affirmations, I am...

Did I accomplish my two main freedom actions today? ☺ 😐 ☹

Did I give a gift and/or minimize? ☺ 😐 ☹

What was it and how did it feel? _____

I meditated for .... **minutes today and I felt:** _____

You are **11**% done with developing your happiness muscle :)

DATE .... / .... / 20 ....

Don't be trapped by dogma - which is living with the results of other people's thinking.
— Steve Jobs

What makes me ☺ ?

What am I thankful for?

Sweet Ass Ideas for:

- -

What are the two **most valuable freedom actions** I will take today to progress toward my vision, goals, and dream life?

1.

2.

What will I **give** and/or **minimize** today?

My **wins** for the day are:

I have an **abundance** of:

What are the two **most valuable freedom actions** I will take tomorrow to progress toward my vision, goals, and dream life?

1.

2.

Nightly Affirmations, I am...

Did I accomplish my two main freedom actions today? ☺ ☺ ☹

Did I give a gift and/or minimize? ☺ ☺ ☹

What was it and how did it feel? _____

I meditated for .... **minutes today and I felt:** _____

You are **12**% done with developing your happiness muscle :)

DATE .... / .... / 20 ....

The next message you need is always right where you are.
– Ram Dass

What makes me ☺ ?

What am I thankful for?

Sweet Ass Ideas for:

- -

What are the two **most valuable freedom actions** I will take today to progress toward my vision, goals, and dream life?

1.

2.

What will I **give** and/or **minimize** today?

My **wins** for the day are:

I have an **abundance** of:

What are the two **most valuable freedom actions** I will take tomorrow to progress toward my vision, goals, and dream life?

1.

2.

Nightly Affirmations, I am...

Did I accomplish my two main freedom actions today? ☺ ☺ ☹

Did I give a gift and/or minimize? ☺ ☺ ☹

What was it and how did it feel? _____

I meditated for .... **minutes today and I felt:** _____

You are **13**% done with developing your happiness muscle :)

There are two mistakes one can make along the road to truth: not going all the way, and not starting.
– Buddha

What makes me ☺ ?

What am I thankful for?

Sweet Ass Ideas for:

What are the two **most valuable freedom actions** I will take today to progress toward my vision, goals, and dream life?

1.

2.

What will I **give** and/or **minimize** today?

My **wins** for the day are:

I have an **abundance** of:

What are the two **most valuable freedom actions** I will take tomorrow to progress toward my vision, goals, and dream life?

1.

2.

Nightly Affirmations, I am...

Did I accomplish my two main freedom actions today? ☺ 😐 ☹

Did I give a gift and/or minimize? ☺ 😐 ☹

What was it and how did it feel? _____

I meditated for .... **minutes today and I felt:** _____

You are **14**% done with developing your happiness muscle :)

DATE .... / .... / 20 ....

Treat everybody like it's their birthday.
– Kid President

What makes me ☺ ?

What am I thankful for?

Sweet Ass Ideas for:

- -

What are the two **most valuable freedom actions** I will take today to progress toward my vision, goals, and dream life?

1.

2.

What will I **give** and/or **minimize** today?

My **wins** for the day are:

I have an **abundance** of:

What are the two **most valuable freedom actions** I will take tomorrow to progress toward my vision, goals, and dream life?

1.

2.

Nightly Affirmations, I am...

Did I accomplish my two main freedom actions today? ☺ ☺ ☹

Did I give a gift and/or minimize? ☺ ☺ ☹

What was it and how did it feel? _____

I meditated for .... **minutes today and I felt:** _____

You are   **15**% done with developing your happiness muscle :)

DATE .... / .... / 20 ....

There is always a reason to complain, and
always a reason to dance. Choose to dance.
– Brad Montague

What makes me ☺ ?

What am I thankful for?

Sweet Ass Ideas for:

- -

What are the two **most valuable freedom actions** I will take today to progress toward my vision, goals, and dream life?

1.

2.

What will I **give** and/or **minimize** today?

My **wins** for the day are:

I have an **abundance** of:

What are the two **most valuable freedom actions** I will take tomorrow to progress toward my vision, goals, and dream life?

1.

2.

Nightly Affirmations, I am...

Did I accomplish my two main freedom actions today? ☺ ☺ ☹

Did I give a gift and/or minimize? ☺ ☺ ☹

What was it and how did it feel? _____

I meditated for .... **minutes today and I felt:** _____

You are   **16**% done with developing your happiness muscle :)

DATE .... / .... / 20 ....

Uncertainty is the gateway to possibility.
– Lissa Rankin

What makes me ☺ ?

What am I thankful for?

Sweet Ass Ideas for:

- -

What are the two **most valuable freedom actions** I will take today to progress toward my vision, goals, and dream life?

1.

2.

What will I **give** and/or **minimize** today?

My **wins** for the day are:

I have an **abundance** of:

What are the two **most valuable freedom actions** I will take tomorrow to progress toward my vision, goals, and dream life?

1.

2.

Nightly Affirmations, I am...

Did I accomplish my two main freedom actions today? ☺ ☺ ☹

Did I give a gift and/or minimize? ☺ ☺ ☹

What was it and how did it feel? _____

I meditated for .... **minutes today and I felt:** _____

You are **17**% done with developing your happiness muscle :)

If we were meant to stay in one place, we'd have roots instead of feet.
— Rachel Wolchin

What makes me ☺ ?

What am I thankful for?

Sweet Ass Ideas for:

What are the two **most valuable freedom actions** I will take today to progress toward my vision, goals, and dream life?

1.

2.

What will I **give** and/or **minimize** today?

My **wins** for the day are:

I have an **abundance** of:

What are the two **most valuable freedom actions** I will take tomorrow to progress toward my vision, goals, and dream life?

1.

2.

Nightly Affirmations, I am...

Did I accomplish my two main freedom actions today?   ☺ ☺ ☹

Did I give a gift and/or minimize?   ☺ ☺ ☹

What was it and how did it feel? _____

I meditated for .... minutes today and I felt: _____

You are   18% done with developing your happiness muscle :)

DATE .... / .... / 20 ....

Conformity is the jailer of freedom and the enemy of growth.
— JFK

What makes me ☺ ?

What am I thankful for?

Sweet Ass Ideas for:

- -

What are the two **most valuable freedom actions** I will take today to progress toward my vision, goals, and dream life?

1.

2.

What will I **give** and/or **minimize** today?

My **wins** for the day are:

I have an **abundance** of:

What are the two **most valuable freedom actions** I will take tomorrow to progress toward my vision, goals, and dream life?

1.

2.

Nightly Affirmations, I am...

Did I accomplish my two main freedom actions today?   ☺ ☺ ☹

Did I give a gift and/or minimize?   ☺ ☺ ☹

What was it and how did it feel? _____

I meditated for .... **minutes today and I felt:** _____

You are   **19** % done with developing your happiness muscle :)

DATE .... / .... / 20 ....

Children, wake up. Hold your mistake up.
– Arcade Fire

What makes me ☺ ?

What am I thankful for?

Sweet Ass Ideas for:

- -

What are the two **most valuable freedom actions** I will take today to progress toward my vision, goals, and dream life?

1.

2.

What will I **give** and/or **minimize** today?

My **wins** for the day are:

I have an **abundance** of:

What are the two **most valuable freedom actions** I will take tomorrow to progress toward my vision, goals, and dream life?

1.

2.

Nightly Affirmations, I am...

Did I accomplish my two main freedom actions today? ☺ ☺ ☹

Did I give a gift and/or minimize? ☺ ☺ ☹

What was it and how did it feel? _____

I meditated for .... **minutes today and I felt:** _____

DATE .... / .... / 20 ....

Walk as if you are kissing the Earth with your feet.
– Thich Nhat Hanh

What makes me ☺ ?

What am I thankful for?

Sweet Ass Ideas for:

- -

What are the two **most valuable freedom actions** I will take today to progress toward my vision, goals, and dream life?

1.

2.

What will I **give** and/or **minimize** today?

My **wins** for the day are:

I have an **abundance** of:

What are the two **most valuable freedom actions** I will take tomorrow to progress toward my vision, goals, and dream life?

1.

2.

Nightly Affirmations, I am...

Did I accomplish my two main freedom actions today? ☺ ☺ ☹

Did I give a gift and/or minimize? ☺ ☺ ☹

What was it and how did it feel? _____

I meditated for .... minutes today and I felt: _____

You are **21%** done with developing your happiness muscle :)

DATE .... / .... / 20 ....

The notes are right under your fingers, you just gotta' take the time out to play the notes. That's life.
— Ray Charles

What makes me ☺ ?

What am I thankful for?

Sweet Ass Ideas for:

- -

What are the two **most valuable freedom actions** I will take today to progress toward my vision, goals, and dream life?

1.

2.

What will I **give** and/or **minimize** today?

My **wins** for the day are:

I have an **abundance** of:

What are the two **most valuable freedom actions** I will take tomorrow to progress toward my vision, goals, and dream life?

1.

2.

Nightly Affirmations, I am...

Did I accomplish my two main freedom actions today? ☺ ☺ ☹

Did I give a gift and/or minimize? ☺ ☺ ☹

What was it and how did it feel? _____

I meditated for .... **minutes today and I felt:** _____

You are **22**% done with developing your happiness muscle :)

DATE .... / .... / 20 ....

I am an old man who has known a great deal of troubles,
most of which never happened.
– Mark Twain

What makes me ☺ ?

What am I thankful for?

Sweet Ass Ideas for:

- -

What are the two **most valuable freedom actions** I will take today to progress toward my vision, goals, and dream life?

1.

2.

What will I **give** and/or **minimize** today?

My **wins** for the day are:

I have an **abundance** of:

What are the two **most valuable freedom actions** I will take tomorrow to progress toward my vision, goals, and dream life?

1.

2.

Nightly Affirmations, I am...

Did I accomplish my two main freedom actions today? ☺ ☺ ☹

Did I give a gift and/or minimize? ☺ ☺ ☹

What was it and how did it feel? _____

I meditated for .... minutes today and I felt: _____

You are **23** % done with developing your happiness muscle :)

DATE .... / .... / 20 ....

Logic will get you from A to B. Imagination will take you everywhere.
– Albert Einstein

What makes me ☺ ?

What am I thankful for?

Sweet Ass Ideas for:

What are the two **most valuable freedom actions** I will take today to progress toward my vision, goals, and dream life?

1.

2.

What will I **give** and/or **minimize** today?

My **wins** for the day are:

I have an **abundance** of:

What are the two **most valuable freedom actions** I will take tomorrow to progress toward my vision, goals, and dream life?

1.

2.

Nightly Affirmations, I am...

Did I accomplish my two main freedom actions today?   ☺ ☺ ☹

Did I give a gift and/or minimize?   ☺ ☺ ☹

What was it and how did it feel? _____

I meditated for .... **minutes today and I felt:** _____

DATE .... / .... / 20 ....

Pain heals, chicks dig scars and glory lasts forever.
– Keanu Reeves

What makes me ☺ ?

What am I thankful for?

Sweet Ass Ideas for:

- -

What are the two **most valuable freedom actions** I will take today to progress toward my vision, goals, and dream life?

1.

2.

What will I **give** and/or **minimize** today?

My **wins** for the day are:

I have an **abundance** of:

What are the two **most valuable freedom actions** I will take tomorrow to progress toward my vision, goals, and dream life?

1.

2.

Nightly Affirmations, I am...

Did I accomplish my two main freedom actions today? ☺ ☺ ☹

Did I give a gift and/or minimize? ☺ ☺ ☹

What was it and how did it feel? _____

I meditated for .... **minutes today and I felt:** _____

You are **25**% done with developing your happiness muscle :)

DATE .... / .... / 20 ....

Let go of like and dislike and let things be.
– Ajahn Chah

What makes me ☺ ?

What am I thankful for?

Sweet Ass Ideas for:

What are the two **most valuable freedom actions** I will take today to progress toward my vision, goals, and dream life?

1.

2.

What will I **give** and/or **minimize** today?

My **wins** for the day are:

I have an **abundance** of:

What are the two **most valuable freedom actions** I will take tomorrow to progress toward my vision, goals, and dream life?

1.

2.

Nightly Affirmations, I am…

Did I accomplish my two main freedom actions today? ☺ ☺ ☹

Did I give a gift and/or minimize? ☺ ☺ ☹

What was it and how did it feel? _____

I meditated for .... **minutes today and I felt:** _____

You are **26**% done with developing your happiness muscle :)

DATE .... / .... / 20 ....

Whichever path you take, make sure it has heart. Do it so you feel it.
— Erik Stenqvist

What makes me ☺ ?

What am I thankful for?

Sweet Ass Ideas for:

- -

What are the two **most valuable freedom actions** I will take today to progress toward my vision, goals, and dream life?

1.

2.

What will I **give** and/or **minimize** today?

My **wins** for the day are:

I have an **abundance** of:

What are the two **most valuable freedom actions** I will take tomorrow to progress toward my vision, goals, and dream life?

1.

2.

Nightly Affirmations, I am...

Did I accomplish my two main freedom actions today? ☺ ☺ ☹

Did I give a gift and/or minimize? ☺ ☺ ☹

What was it and how did it feel? _____

I meditated for .... **minutes today and I felt:** _____

You are **27**% done with developing your happiness muscle :)

Most of us have two lives. The life we live, and the unlived life within us. Between the two stands Resistance.
– Steven Pressfield

What makes me ☺ ?

What am I thankful for?

Sweet Ass Ideas for:

- -

What are the two **most valuable freedom actions** I will take today to progress toward my vision, goals, and dream life?

1.

2.

What will I **give** and/or **minimize** today?

My **wins** for the day are:

I have an **abundance** of:

What are the two **most valuable freedom actions** I will take tomorrow to progress toward my vision, goals, and dream life?

1.

2.

Nightly Affirmations, I am...

Did I accomplish my two main freedom actions today? ☺ 😐 ☹

Did I give a gift and/or minimize? ☺ 😐 ☹

What was it and how did it feel? _____

I meditated for .... **minutes today and I felt:** _____

You are **28**% done with developing your happiness muscle :)

*Meditate, visualize and create your own reality and the
universe will simply reflect back to you.*
– Amit Ray

What makes me ☺ ?

What am I thankful for?

Sweet Ass Ideas for:

- -

What are the two **most valuable freedom
actions** I will take today to progress
toward my vision, goals, and dream life?

1.

2.

What will I **give** and/or **minimize** today?

My **wins** for the day are:

I have an **abundance** of:

What are the two **most valuable freedom actions** I will take tomorrow to progress toward my vision, goals, and dream life?

1.

2.

Nightly Affirmations, I am...

Did I accomplish my two main freedom actions today? ☺ ☺ ☹

Did I give a gift and/or minimize? ☺ ☺ ☹

What was it and how did it feel? _____

I meditated for .... **minutes today and I felt:** _____

You are **29**% done with developing your happiness muscle :)

DATE .... / .... / 20 ....

Treat everyone you meet like God in drag.
– Ram Dass

What makes me ☺ ?

What am I thankful for?

Sweet Ass Ideas for:

What are the two **most valuable freedom actions** I will take today to progress toward my vision, goals, and dream life?

1.

2.

What will I **give** and/or **minimize** today?

My **wins** for the day are:

I have an **abundance** of:

What are the two **most valuable freedom actions** I will take tomorrow to progress toward my vision, goals, and dream life?

1.

2.

Nightly Affirmations, I am...

Did I accomplish my two main freedom actions today? ☺ ☺ ☹

Did I give a gift and/or minimize? ☺ ☺ ☹

What was it and how did it feel? _____

I meditated for .... **minutes today and I felt:** _____

You are **30**% done with developing your happiness muscle :)

DATE .... / .... / 20 ....

Everyone thinks of changing the world,
but no one thinks of changing himself.
– Leo Tolstoy

What makes me ☺ ?

What am I thankful for?

Sweet Ass Ideas for:

- -

What are the two **most valuable freedom actions** I will take today to progress toward my vision, goals, and dream life?

1.

2.

What will I **give** and/or **minimize** today?

My **wins** for the day are:

I have an **abundance** of:

What are the two **most valuable freedom actions** I will take tomorrow to progress toward my vision, goals, and dream life?

1.

2.

Nightly Affirmations, I am...

Did I accomplish my two main freedom actions today? ☺ ☺ ☹

Did I give a gift and/or minimize? ☺ ☺ ☹

What was it and how did it feel? _____

I meditated for .... **minutes today and I felt:** _____

DATE .... / .... / 20 ....

It is not enough to be busy. So are the ants.
The question is: What are we busy about?
– Henry David Thoreau

What makes me ☺ ?

What am I thankful for?

Sweet Ass Ideas for:

What are the two **most valuable freedom actions** I will take today to progress toward my vision, goals, and dream life?

1.

2.

What will I **give** and/or **minimize** today?

My **wins** for the day are:

I have an **abundance** of:

What are the two **most valuable freedom actions** I will take tomorrow to progress toward my vision, goals, and dream life?

1.

2.

Nightly Affirmations, I am...

Did I accomplish my two main freedom actions today? ☺ 😐 ☹

Did I give a gift and/or minimize? ☺ 😐 ☹

What was it and how did it feel? _____

I meditated for .... **minutes today and I felt:** _____

You are **32**% done with developing your happiness muscle :)

DATE ………… / ………… / 20 ………

If we take care of the minutes, the years will take care of themselves.
– Ben Franklin

What makes me ☺ ?

What am I thankful for?

Sweet Ass Ideas for:

- -

What are the two **most valuable freedom actions** I will take today to progress toward my vision, goals, and dream life?

1.

2.

What will I **give** and/or **minimize** today?

My **wins** for the day are:

I have an **abundance** of:

What are the two **most valuable freedom actions** I will take tomorrow to progress toward my vision, goals, and dream life?

1.

2.

Nightly Affirmations, I am...

Did I accomplish my two main freedom actions today? ☺ ☺ ☹

Did I give a gift and/or minimize? ☺ ☺ ☹

What was it and how did it feel? _____

I meditated for .... **minutes today and I felt:** _____

You are   **33**% done with developing your happiness muscle :)

DATE .... / .... / 20 ....

Live your life as if you have to live it over again.
– Heath Armstrong

What makes me ☺ ?

What am I thankful for?

Sweet Ass Ideas for:

- -

What are the two **most valuable freedom actions** I will take today to progress toward my vision, goals, and dream life?

1.

2.

What will I **give** and/or **minimize** today?

142

My **wins** for the day are:

I have an **abundance** of:

What are the two **most valuable freedom actions** I will take tomorrow to progress toward my vision, goals, and dream life?

1.

2.

Nightly Affirmations, I am…

Did I accomplish my two main freedom actions today? ☺ 😐 ☹

Did I give a gift and/or minimize? ☺ 😐 ☹

What was it and how did it feel? _____

I meditated for .... **minutes today and I felt:** _____

You are **34**% done with developing your happiness muscle :)

DATE .... / .... / 20 ....

Create like a god, command like a king and work like a slave.
— Constantin Brâncuși

What makes me ☺ ?

What am I thankful for?

Sweet Ass Ideas for:

- -

What are the two **most valuable freedom actions** I will take today to progress toward my vision, goals, and dream life?

1.

2.

What will I **give** and/or **minimize** today?

My **wins** for the day are:

I have an **abundance** of:

What are the two **most valuable freedom actions** I will take tomorrow to progress toward my vision, goals, and dream life?

1.

2.

Nightly Affirmations, I am...

Did I accomplish my two main freedom actions today? ☺ ☺ ☹

Did I give a gift and/or minimize? ☺ ☺ ☹

What was it and how did it feel? _____

I meditated for .... minutes today and I felt: _____

You are **35**% done with developing your happiness muscle :)

On the field of the self stand a knight and a dragon.
You are the knight and resistance is the dragon.
— Steven Pressfield

What makes me ☺ ?

What am I thankful for?

Sweet Ass Ideas for:

What are the two **most valuable freedom actions** I will take today to progress toward my vision, goals, and dream life?

1.

2.

What will I **give** and/or **minimize** today?

My **wins** for the day are:

I have an **abundance** of:

What are the two **most valuable freedom actions** I will take tomorrow to progress toward my vision, goals, and dream life?

1.

2.

Nightly Affirmations, I am...

Did I accomplish my two main freedom actions today?　☺ ☺ ☹

Did I give a gift and/or minimize?　☺ ☺ ☹

What was it and how did it feel? _____

I meditated for .... minutes today and I felt: _____

You are **36**% done with developing your happiness muscle :)

DATE .... / .... / 20 ....

What we have done for ourselves dies within us. What we have done for others and the world remains and is immortal.
– Albert Pike

What makes me ☺ ?

What am I thankful for?

Sweet Ass Ideas for:

What are the two **most valuable freedom actions** I will take today to progress toward my vision, goals, and dream life?

1.

2.

What will I **give** and/or **minimize** today?

My **wins** for the day are:

I have an **abundance** of:

What are the two **most valuable freedom actions** I will take tomorrow to progress toward my vision, goals, and dream life?

1.

2.

Nightly Affirmations, I am...

Did I accomplish my two main freedom actions today? 😊 😐 ☹️

Did I give a gift and/or minimize? 😊 😐 ☹️

What was it and how did it feel? _____

I meditated for .... **minutes today and I felt:** _____

You are **37**% done with developing your happiness muscle :)

DATE .... / .... / 20 ....

Be like a lotus. Let the beauty of your heart speak.
Be grateful to the mud, water, air and the light.
– Amit Ray

What makes me ☺ ?

What am I thankful for?

Sweet Ass Ideas for:

What are the two **most valuable freedom actions** I will take today to progress toward my vision, goals, and dream life?

1.

2.

What will I **give** and/or **minimize** today?

My **wins** for the day are:

I have an **abundance** of:

What are the two **most valuable freedom actions** I will take tomorrow to progress toward my vision, goals, and dream life?

1.

2.

Nightly Affirmations, I am...

Did I accomplish my two main freedom actions today? ☺ ☺ ☹

Did I give a gift and/or minimize? ☺ ☺ ☹

What was it and how did it feel? _____

I meditated for .... **minutes today and I felt:** _____

You are **38**% done with developing your happiness muscle :)

There are only two ways to live your life. One is as though nothing is a miracle. The other is as though everything is a miracle.
– Albert Einstein

What makes me ☺ ?

What am I thankful for?

Sweet Ass Ideas for:

- -

What are the two **most valuable freedom actions** I will take today to progress toward my vision, goals, and dream life?

1.

2.

What will I **give** and/or **minimize** today?

My **wins** for the day are:

I have an **abundance** of:

What are the two **most valuable freedom actions** I will take tomorrow to progress toward my vision, goals, and dream life?

1.

2.

Nightly Affirmations, I am...

Did I accomplish my two main freedom actions today? ☺ ☺ ☹

Did I give a gift and/or minimize? ☺ ☺ ☹

What was it and how did it feel? _____

I meditated for .... **minutes today and I felt:** _____

DATE .... / .... / 20 ....

What really frightens and dismays us is not external events themselves, but the way in which we think about them. It is not things that disturb us, but our interpretation of their significance. – Epictetus

What makes me ☺ ?

What am I thankful for?

Sweet Ass Ideas for:

- -

What are the two **most valuable freedom actions** I will take today to progress toward my vision, goals, and dream life?

1.

2.

What will I **give** and/or **minimize** today?

My **wins** for the day are:

I have an **abundance** of:

What are the two **most valuable freedom actions** I will take tomorrow to progress toward my vision, goals, and dream life?

1.

2.

Nightly Affirmations, I am...

Did I accomplish my two main freedom actions today? ☺ ☺ ☹

Did I give a gift and/or minimize? ☺ ☺ ☹

What was it and how did it feel? _____

I meditated for .... **minutes today and I felt:** _____

You are **40**% done with developing your happiness muscle :)

DATE .... / .... / 20 ....

Our deepest fear is not that we are inadequate, but that we are powerful beyond measure. It is our light, not our darkness, that most frightens us.
– Marianne Williamson

What makes me ☺ ?

What am I thankful for?

Sweet Ass Ideas for:

What are the two **most valuable freedom actions** I will take today to progress toward my vision, goals, and dream life?

1.

2.

What will I **give** and/or **minimize** today?

My **wins** for the day are:

I have an **abundance** of:

What are the two **most valuable freedom actions** I will take tomorrow to progress toward my vision, goals, and dream life?

1.

2.

Nightly Affirmations, I am...

Did I accomplish my two main freedom actions today? ☺ ☻ ☹

Did I give a gift and/or minimize? ☺ ☻ ☹

What was it and how did it feel? _____

I meditated for .... **minutes today and I felt:** _____

You are 41% done with developing your happiness muscle :)

DATE ………… / ………… / 20 …………

Do every act of your life as though it were the very last act of your life.
– Marcus Aurelius

What makes me ☺ ?

What am I thankful for?

Sweet Ass Ideas for:

- -

What are the two **most valuable freedom actions** I will take today to progress toward my vision, goals, and dream life?

1.

2.

What will I **give** and/or **minimize** today?

My **wins** for the day are:

I have an **abundance** of:

What are the two **most valuable freedom actions** I will take tomorrow to progress toward my vision, goals, and dream life?

1.

2.

Nightly Affirmations, I am...

Did I accomplish my two main freedom actions today? ☺ ☺ ☹

Did I give a gift and/or minimize? ☺ ☺ ☹

What was it and how did it feel? _____

I meditated for .... **minutes today and I felt:** _____

You are **42**% done with developing your happiness muscle :)

DATE .... / .... / 20 ....

Happiness is the absence of the striving for happiness.
– Chuang Tzu

What makes me ☺ ?

What am I thankful for?

Sweet Ass Ideas for:

- -

What are the two **most valuable freedom actions** I will take today to progress toward my vision, goals, and dream life?

1.

2.

What will I **give** and/or **minimize** today?

My **wins** for the day are:

I have an **abundance** of:

What are the two **most valuable freedom actions** I will take tomorrow to progress toward my vision, goals, and dream life?

1.

2.

Nightly Affirmations, I am...

Did I accomplish my two main freedom actions today? ☺ ☺ ☹

Did I give a gift and/or minimize? ☺ ☺ ☹

What was it and how did it feel? _____

I meditated for .... **minutes today and I felt:** _____

You are **43**% done with developing your happiness muscle :)

DATE .... / .... / 20 ....

Do not ruin today with mourning tomorrow.
— Catherynne M. Valente

What makes me ☺ ?

What am I thankful for?

Sweet Ass Ideas for:

- -

What are the two **most valuable freedom actions** I will take today to progress toward my vision, goals, and dream life?

1.

2.

What will I **give** and/or **minimize** today?

My **wins** for the day are:

I have an **abundance** of:

What are the two **most valuable freedom actions** I will take tomorrow to progress toward my vision, goals, and dream life?

1.

2.

Nightly Affirmations, I am...

Did I accomplish my two main freedom actions today? ☺ ☺ ☹

Did I give a gift and/or minimize? ☺ ☺ ☹

What was it and how did it feel? _____

I meditated for .... **minutes today and I felt:** _____

You are 44% done with developing your happiness muscle :)

DATE .... / .... / 20 ....

The more silent you become, the better you will hear.
– Ram Dass

What makes me ☺ ?

What am I thankful for?

Sweet Ass Ideas for:

What are the two **most valuable freedom actions** I will take today to progress toward my vision, goals, and dream life?

1.

2.

What will I **give** and/or **minimize** today?

My **wins** for the day are:

I have an **abundance** of:

What are the two **most valuable freedom actions** I will take tomorrow to progress toward my vision, goals, and dream life?

1.

2.

Nightly Affirmations, I am...

Did I accomplish my two main freedom actions today? ☺ ☺ ☹

Did I give a gift and/or minimize? ☺ ☺ ☹

What was it and how did it feel? _____

I meditated for .... **minutes today and I felt:** _____

You are **45** % done with developing your happiness muscle :)

DATE ………. / ………. / 20 ………

You're alive. If that's not something to smile about,
then I don't know what is.
– Chad Sugg

What makes me ☺ ?

What am I thankful for?

Sweet Ass Ideas for:

- -

What are the two **most valuable freedom actions** I will take today to progress toward my vision, goals, and dream life?

1.

2.

What will I **give** and/or **minimize** today?

My **wins** for the day are:

I have an **abundance** of:

What are the two **most valuable freedom actions** I will take tomorrow to progress toward my vision, goals, and dream life?

1.

2.

Nightly Affirmations, I am...

Did I accomplish my two main freedom actions today? ☺ ☺ ☹

Did I give a gift and/or minimize? ☺ ☺ ☹

What was it and how did it feel? _____

I meditated for .... **minutes today and I felt:** _____

You are **46**% done with developing your happiness muscle :)

DATE .... / .... / 20 ....

*Emotions are like waves. Watch them disappear in the
distance on the vast calm ocean.*
– Ram Dass

What makes me ☺ ?

What am I thankful for?

Sweet Ass Ideas for:

What are the two **most valuable freedom
actions** I will take today to progress
toward my vision, goals, and dream life?

1.

2.

What will I **give** and/or **minimize** today?

My **wins** for the day are:

I have an **abundance** of:

What are the two **most valuable freedom actions** I will take tomorrow to progress toward my vision, goals, and dream life?

1.

2.

Nightly Affirmations, I am...

Did I accomplish my two main freedom actions today? ☺ ☺ ☹

Did I give a gift and/or minimize? ☺ ☺ ☹

What was it and how did it feel? _____

I meditated for .... **minutes today and I felt:** _____

You are   **47**% done with developing your happiness muscle :)

DATE .... / .... / 20 ....

Life isn't about waiting for the storm to pass.
It's about learning to dance in the rain.
– Vivian Greene

What makes me ☺ ?

What am I thankful for?

Sweet Ass Ideas for:

- -

What are the two **most valuable freedom actions** I will take today to progress toward my vision, goals, and dream life?

1.

2.

What will I **give** and/or **minimize** today?

My **wins** for the day are:

I have an **abundance** of:

What are the two **most valuable freedom actions** I will take tomorrow to progress toward my vision, goals, and dream life?

1.

2.

Nightly Affirmations, I am...

Did I accomplish my two main freedom actions today? ☺ ☺ ☹

Did I give a gift and/or minimize? ☺ ☺ ☹

What was it and how did it feel? _____

I meditated for .... minutes today and I felt: _____

You are **48**% done with developing your happiness muscle :)

DATE .... / .... / 20 ....

A pessimist sees the difficulty in every opportunity;
an optimist sees the opportunity in every difficulty.
– Winston Churchill

What makes me ☺ ?

What am I thankful for?

Sweet Ass Ideas for:

What are the two **most valuable freedom actions** I will take today to progress toward my vision, goals, and dream life?

1.

2.

What will I **give** and/or **minimize** today?

My **wins** for the day are:

I have an **abundance** of:

What are the two **most valuable freedom actions** I will take tomorrow to progress toward my vision, goals, and dream life?

1.

2.

Nightly Affirmations, I am...

Did I accomplish my two main freedom actions today? ☺ ☺ ☹

Did I give a gift and/or minimize? ☺ ☺ ☹

What was it and how did it feel? _____

I meditated for .... **minutes today and I felt:** _____

You are **49**% done with developing your happiness muscle :)

DATE .... / .... / 20 ....

Whether you think you can, or think you can't — you're right.
— Henry Ford

What makes me ☺ ?

What am I thankful for?

Sweet Ass Ideas for:

- -

What are the two **most valuable freedom actions** I will take today to progress toward my vision, goals, and dream life?

1.

2.

What will I **give** and/or **minimize** today?

My **wins** for the day are:

I have an **abundance** of:

What are the two **most valuable freedom actions** I will take tomorrow to progress toward my vision, goals, and dream life?

1.

2.

Nightly Affirmations, I am…

Did I accomplish my two main freedom actions today? ☺ ☺ ☹

Did I give a gift and/or minimize? ☺ ☺ ☹

What was it and how did it feel? _____

I meditated for .... **minutes today and I felt:** _____

You are **50** % done with developing your happiness muscle :)

DATE .... / .... / 20 ....

It's hard to beat a person who never gives up.
– Babe Ruth

What makes me ☺ ?

What am I thankful for?

Sweet Ass Ideas for:

- -

What are the two **most valuable freedom actions** I will take today to progress toward my vision, goals, and dream life?

1.

2.

What will I **give** and/or **minimize** today?

My **wins** for the day are:

I have an **abundance** of:

What are the two **most valuable freedom actions** I will take tomorrow to progress toward my vision, goals, and dream life?

1.

2.

Nightly Affirmations, I am...

Did I accomplish my two main freedom actions today? ☺ ☺ ☹

Did I give a gift and/or minimize? ☺ ☺ ☹

What was it and how did it feel? _____

I meditated for .... minutes today and I felt: _____

You are **51**% done with developing your happiness muscle :)

DATE .... / .... / 20 ....

Be happy in the moment, that's enough.
Each moment is all we need, not more.
– Mother Teresa

What makes me ☺ ?

What am I thankful for?

Sweet Ass Ideas for:

What are the two **most valuable freedom actions** I will take today to progress toward my vision, goals, and dream life?

1.

2.

What will I **give** and/or **minimize** today?

My **wins** for the day are:

I have an **abundance** of:

What are the two **most valuable freedom actions** I will take tomorrow to progress toward my vision, goals, and dream life?

1.

2.

Nightly Affirmations, I am...

Did I accomplish my two main freedom actions today? ☺ ☺ ☹

Did I give a gift and/or minimize? ☺ ☺ ☹

What was it and how did it feel? _____

I meditated for .... **minutes today and I felt:** _____

You are **52**% done with developing your happiness muscle :)

DATE .... / .... / 20 ....

Strive not to be a success, but rather to be of value.
— Albert Einstein

What makes me ☺ ?

What am I thankful for?

Sweet Ass Ideas for:

- -

What are the two **most valuable freedom actions** I will take today to progress toward my vision, goals, and dream life?

1.

2.

What will I **give** and/or **minimize** today?

My **wins** for the day are:

I have an **abundance** of:

What are the two **most valuable freedom actions** I will take tomorrow to progress toward my vision, goals, and dream life?

1.

2.

Nightly Affirmations, I am...

Did I accomplish my two main freedom actions today? ☺ 😐 ☹

Did I give a gift and/or minimize? ☺ 😐 ☹

What was it and how did it feel? _____

I meditated for .... minutes today and I felt: _____

You are **53**% done with developing your happiness muscle :)

DATE .... / .... / 20 ....

No army can withstand the strength of an idea whose time has come.
– Victor Hugo

What makes me ☺ ?

What am I thankful for?

Sweet Ass Ideas for:

What are the two **most valuable freedom actions** I will take today to progress toward my vision, goals, and dream life?

1.

2.

What will I **give** and/or **minimize** today?

My **wins** for the day are:

I have an **abundance** of:

What are the two **most valuable freedom actions** I will take tomorrow to progress toward my vision, goals, and dream life?

1.

2.

Nightly Affirmations, I am...

Did I accomplish my two main freedom actions today?   ☺ ☺ ☹

Did I give a gift and/or minimize?   ☺ ☺ ☹

What was it and how did it feel? _____

I meditated for .... minutes today and I felt: _____

You are   **54**% done with developing your happiness muscle :)

DATE .... / .... / 20 ....

Detachment results it clarity; clarity expresses itself in love.
– Tao Te Ching

What makes me ☺ ?

What am I thankful for?

Sweet Ass Ideas for:

- -

What are the two **most valuable freedom actions** I will take today to progress toward my vision, goals, and dream life?

1.

2.

What will I **give** and/or **minimize** today?

My **wins** for the day are:

I have an **abundance** of:

What are the two **most valuable freedom actions** I will take tomorrow to progress toward my vision, goals, and dream life?

1.

2.

Nightly Affirmations, I am...

Did I accomplish my two main freedom actions today? ☺ ☺ ☹

Did I give a gift and/or minimize? ☺ ☺ ☹

What was it and how did it feel? _____

I meditated for .... minutes today and I felt: _____

You are **55**% done with developing your happiness muscle :)

DATE ………… / ………… / 20 …………

If you are distressed by anything external, the pain is not due to the thing itself, but to your estimate of it; and this you have the power to revoke at any moment. – Marcus Aurelius

What makes me ☺ ?

What am I thankful for?

Sweet Ass Ideas for:

What are the two **most valuable freedom actions** I will take today to progress toward my vision, goals, and dream life?

1.

2.

What will I **give** and/or **minimize** today?

My **wins** for the day are:

I have an **abundance** of:

What are the two **most valuable freedom actions** I will take tomorrow
to progress toward my vision, goals, and dream life?

1.

2.

Nightly Affirmations, I am...

Did I accomplish my two main freedom actions today?   ☺ ☺ ☹

Did I give a gift and/or minimize?   ☺ ☺ ☹

What was it and how did it feel? _____

I meditated for .... **minutes today and I felt:** _____

You are   **56**% done with developing your happiness muscle :)

DATE .... / .... / 20 ....

Until we have begun to go without them, we fail to realize how unnecessary many things are. We've been using them not because we needed them but because we had them. – Seneca

What makes me ☺ ?

What am I thankful for?

Sweet Ass Ideas for:

- -

What are the two **most valuable freedom actions** I will take today to progress toward my vision, goals, and dream life?

1.

2.

What will I **give** and/or **minimize** today?

My **wins** for the day are:

I have an **abundance** of:

What are the two **most valuable freedom actions** I will take tomorrow to progress toward my vision, goals, and dream life?

1.

2.

Nightly Affirmations, I am...

Did I accomplish my two main freedom actions today? ☺ ☺ ☹

Did I give a gift and/or minimize? ☺ ☺ ☹

What was it and how did it feel? _____

I meditated for .... **minutes today and I felt:** _____

You are **57**% done with developing your happiness muscle :)

DATE .... / .... / 20 ....

If you want to find God, hang out in the space between your thoughts.
– Alan Cohen

What makes me ☺ ?

What am I thankful for?

Sweet Ass Ideas for:

- -

What are the two **most valuable freedom actions** I will take today to progress toward my vision, goals, and dream life?

1.

2.

What will I **give** and/or **minimize** today?

My **wins** for the day are:

I have an **abundance** of:

What are the two **most valuable freedom actions** I will take tomorrow to progress toward my vision, goals, and dream life?

1.

2.

Nightly Affirmations, I am...

Did I accomplish my two main freedom actions today? ☺ ☺ ☹

Did I give a gift and/or minimize? ☺ ☺ ☹

What was it and how did it feel? _____

I meteditated for .... minutes today and I felt: _____

You are   58% done with developing your happiness muscle :)

DATE .... / .... / 20 ....

You should not be carried away by the dictation of the mind,
but the mind should be carried by your dictation.
– A.C Bhaktivedanta Swami

What makes me ☺ ?

What am I thankful for?

Sweet Ass Ideas for:

- -

What are the two **most valuable freedom actions** I will take today to progress toward my vision, goals, and dream life?

1.

2.

What will I **give** and/or **minimize** today?

My **wins** for the day are:

I have an **abundance** of:

What are the two **most valuable freedom actions** I will take tomorrow to progress toward my vision, goals, and dream life?

1.

2.

Nightly Affirmations, I am...

Did I accomplish my two main freedom actions today?   ☺ ☺ ☹

Did I give a gift and/or minimize?   ☺ ☺ ☹

What was it and how did it feel? _____

I meditated for .... minutes today and I felt: _____

You are   **59**% done with developing your happiness muscle :)

DATE .... / .... / 20 ....

Your worst enemy cannot harm you as much
as your own thoughts, unguarded.
– Buddha

What makes me ☺ ?

What am I thankful for?

Sweet Ass Ideas for:

- -

What are the two **most valuable freedom actions** I will take today to progress toward my vision, goals, and dream life?

1.

2.

What will I **give** and/or **minimize** today?

My **wins** for the day are:

I have an **abundance** of:

What are the two **most valuable freedom actions** I will take tomorrow to progress toward my vision, goals, and dream life?

1.

2.

Nightly Affirmations, I am...

Did I accomplish my two main freedom actions today? ☺ 😐 ☹

Did I give a gift and/or minimize? ☺ 😐 ☹

What was it and how did it feel? _____

I meditated for .... **minutes today and I felt:** _____

You are **60**% done with developing your happiness muscle :)

DATE .... / .... / 20 ....

Be here now. Be someplace else later. Is that so complicated?
– David M. Bader

What makes me ☺ ?

What am I thankful for?

Sweet Ass Ideas for:

- -

What are the two **most valuable freedom actions** I will take today to progress toward my vision, goals, and dream life?

1.

2.

What will I **give** and/or **minimize** today?

My **wins** for the day are:

I have an **abundance** of:

What are the two **most valuable freedom actions** I will take tomorrow to progress toward my vision, goals, and dream life?

1.

2.

Nightly Affirmations, I am...

Did I accomplish my two main freedom actions today? ☺ ☺ ☹

Did I give a gift and/or minimize? ☺ ☺ ☹

What was it and how did it feel? _____

I meditated for .... minutes today and I felt: _____

You are **61**% done with developing your happiness muscle :)

DATE .... / .... / 20 ....

If you ever start taking things too seriously, just remember that we are talking monkeys on an organic spaceship flying through the universe.
– Joe Rogan

What makes me ☺ ?

What am I thankful for?

Sweet Ass Ideas for:

What are the two **most valuable freedom actions** I will take today to progress toward my vision, goals, and dream life?

1.

2.

What will I **give** and/or **minimize** today?

My **wins** for the day are:

I have an **abundance** of:

What are the two **most valuable freedom actions** I will take tomorrow to progress toward my vision, goals, and dream life?

1.

2.

Nightly Affirmations, I am...

Did I accomplish my two main freedom actions today? ☺ ☺ ☹

Did I give a gift and/or minimize? ☺ ☺ ☹

What was it and how did it feel? _____

I meditated for .... minutes today and I felt: _____

You are **62**% done with developing your happiness muscle :)

DATE .... / .... / 20 ....

*There **are as** many atoms in a single molecule of your DNA as there are stars in the typical galaxy. We are, each of us, a little universe.*
– Neil deGrasse Tyson

What makes me ☺ ?

What am I thankful for?

Sweet Ass Ideas for:

- -

What are the two **most valuable freedom actions** I will take today to progress toward my vision, goals, and dream life?

1.

2.

.

What will I **give** and/or **minimize** today?

My **wins** for the day are:

I have an **abundance** of:

What are the two **most valuable freedom actions** I will take tomorrow
to progress toward my vision, goals, and dream life?

1.

2.

Nightly Affirmations, I am...

Did I accomplish my two main freedom actions today? ☺ ☺ ☹

Did I give a gift and/or minimize? ☺ ☺ ☹

What was it and how did it feel? _____

I meditated for .... **minutes today and I felt:** _____

You are **63**% done with developing your happiness muscle :)

DATE ………… / ………… / 20 …………

If we only arrive to worship the sunset,
the Heavens will grant us another to see.
– Heath Armstrong

What makes me ☺ ?

What am I thankful for?

Sweet Ass Ideas for:

What are the two **most valuable freedom actions** I will take today to progress toward my vision, goals, and dream life?

1.

2.

What will I **give** and/or **minimize** today?

My **wins** for the day are:

I have an **abundance** of:

What are the two **most valuable freedom actions** I will take tomorrow
to progress toward my vision, goals, and dream life?

1.

2.

Nightly Affirmations, I am...

Did I accomplish my two main freedom actions today? ☺ ☺ ☹

Did I give a gift and/or minimize? ☺ ☺ ☹

What was it and how did it feel? _____

I meditated for .... **minutes today and I felt:** _____

DATE .... / .... / 20 ....

Every strike brings me closer to the next home run.
— Babe Ruth

What makes me ☺ ?

What am I thankful for?

Sweet Ass Ideas for:

What are the two **most valuable freedom actions** I will take today to progress toward my vision, goals, and dream life?

1.

2.

What will I **give** and/or **minimize** today?

My **wins** for the day are:

I have an **abundance** of:

What are the two **most valuable freedom actions** I will take tomorrow to progress toward my vision, goals, and dream life?

1.

2.

Nightly Affirmations, I am...

Did I accomplish my two main freedom actions today? ☺ ☺ ☹

Did I give a gift and/or minimize? ☺ ☺ ☹

What was it and how did it feel? _____

I meditated for .... **minutes today and I felt:** _____

You are **65%** done with developing your happiness muscle :)

DATE .... / .... / 20 ....

A journey of a thousand miles begins with a single step.
— Lao Tzu

What makes me ☺ ?

What am I thankful for?

Sweet Ass Ideas for:

- -

What are the two **most valuable freedom actions** I will take today to progress toward my vision, goals, and dream life?

1.

2.

What will I **give** and/or **minimize** today?

My **wins** for the day are:

I have an **abundance** of:

What are the two **most valuable freedom actions** I will take tomorrow to progress toward my vision, goals, and dream life?

1.

2.

Nightly Affirmations, I am...

Did I accomplish my two main freedom actions today?   ☺ ☺ ☹

Did I give a gift and/or minimize?   ☺ ☺ ☹

What was it and how did it feel? _____

I meditated for .... minutes today and I felt: _____

You are   **66**% done with developing your happiness muscle :)

DATE .... / .... / 20 ....

A man who dares to waste one hour of life
has not discovered the value of life.
– Charles Darwin

What makes me 😊 ?

What am I thankful for?

Sweet Ass Ideas for:

What are the two **most valuable freedom actions** I will take today to progress toward my vision, goals, and dream life?

1.

2.

What will I **give** and/or **minimize** today?

My **wins** for the day are:

I have an **abundance** of:

What are the two **most valuable freedom actions** I will take tomorrow to progress toward my vision, goals, and dream life?

1.

2.

Nightly Affirmations, I am...

Did I accomplish my two main freedom actions today? ☺ 😐 ☹

Did I give a gift and/or minimize? ☺ 😐 ☹

What was it and how did it feel? _____

I meditated for .... **minutes today and I felt:** _____

You are   **67**% done with developing your happiness muscle :)

DATE .... / .... / 20 ....

Shoot for the moon. Even if you miss, you'll land among the stars.
– Les Brown

What makes me ☺ ?

What am I thankful for?

Sweet Ass Ideas for:

What are the two **most valuable freedom actions** I will take today to progress toward my vision, goals, and dream life?

1.

2.

What will I **give** and/or **minimize** today?

My **wins** for the day are:

I have an **abundance** of:

What are the two **most valuable freedom actions** I will take tomorrow to progress toward my vision, goals, and dream life?

1.

2.

Nightly Affirmations, I am...

Did I accomplish my two main freedom actions today? ☺ ☺ ☹

Did I give a gift and/or minimize? ☺ ☺ ☹

What was it and how did it feel? _____

I meditated for .... **minutes today and I felt:** _____

You are   **68**% done with developing your happiness muscle :)

DATE .... / .... / 20 ....

*The two most important days in your life are the day
you are born and the day you find out why.*
– Mark Twain

What makes me ☺ ?

What am I thankful for?

Sweet Ass Ideas for:

- -

What are the two **most valuable freedom
actions** I will take today to progress
toward my vision, goals, and dream life?

1.

2.

What will I **give** and/or **minimize** today?

My **wins** for the day are:

I have an **abundance** of:

What are the two **most valuable freedom actions** I will take tomorrow to progress toward my vision, goals, and dream life?

1.

2.

Nightly Affirmations, I am...

Did I accomplish my two main freedom actions today? ☺ ☺ ☹

Did I give a gift and/or minimize? ☺ ☺ ☹

What was it and how did it feel? _____

I meditated for .... **minutes today and I felt:** _____

You are **69**% done with developing your happiness muscle :)

DATE .... / .... / 20 ....

We cannot teach people anything.
We can only help them discover it within themselves.
– Galileo Galilei

What makes me ☺ ?

What am I thankful for?

Sweet Ass Ideas for:

What are the two **most valuable freedom actions** I will take today to progress toward my vision, goals, and dream life?

1.

2.

What will I **give** and/or **minimize** today?

My **wins** for the day are:

I have an **abundance** of:

What are the two **most valuable freedom actions** I will take tomorrow
to progress toward my vision, goals, and dream life?

1.

2.

Nightly Affirmations, I am...

Did I accomplish my two main freedom actions today? ☺ ☺ ☹

Did I give a gift and/or minimize? ☺ ☺ ☹

What was it and how did it feel? _____

I meditated for .... **minutes today and I felt:** _____

You are **70**% done with developing your happiness muscle :)

Yo!
You are **70%** done with your

100 DAYS OF DEVELOPING YOUR HAPPINESS MUSCLE!

Make sure you order your new journal soon so that you can continue to build your momentum!

Also, consider gifting it to someone awesome you know, and watch the magic unfold in both your lives! It's great to have an accountability partner to share these sweet ass experiences with.

You can find the journal on **Amazon.com**, or at **www.sweetassjournal.com**

Don't forget the **FREE BONUS** resources at **www.sweetassjournal.com/bonus**

*"Things turn out the best for those that make
the best of the way things turn out.
– John Wooden*

What makes me ☺ ?

What am I thankful for?

Sweet Ass Ideas for:

What are the two **most valuable freedom actions** I will take today to progress toward my vision, goals, and dream life?

1.

2.

What will I **give** and/or **minimize** today?

My **wins** for the day are:

I have an **abundance** of:

What are the two **most valuable freedom actions** I will take tomorrow to progress toward my vision, goals, and dream life?

1.

2.

Nightly Affirmations, I am...

Did I accomplish my two main freedom actions today? ☺ ☻ ☹

Did I give a gift and/or minimize? ☺ ☻ ☹

What was it and how did it feel? _____

I meditated for .... **minutes today and I felt:** _____

You are **71**% done with developing your happiness muscle :)

DATE .... / .... / 20 ....

There is nothing wrong with hard work. If you are cleaning toilets,
clean the hell out of those toilets!
— Nancie Kang

What makes me ☺ ?

What am I thankful for?

Sweet Ass Ideas for:

- -

What are the two **most valuable freedom actions** I will take today to progress toward my vision, goals, and dream life?

1.

2.

What will I **give** and/or **minimize** today?

My **wins** for the day are:

I have an **abundance** of:

What are the two **most valuable freedom actions** I will take tomorrow to progress toward my vision, goals, and dream life?

1.

2.

Nightly Affirmations, I am...

Did I accomplish my two main freedom actions today? ☺ ☺ ☹

Did I give a gift and/or minimize? ☺ ☺ ☹

What was it and how did it feel? _____

I meditated for .... **minutes today and I felt:** _____

You are **72**% done with developing your happiness muscle :)

DATE .... / .... / 20 ....

Live the life you have while you create the life of your dreams.
– Hal Elrod

What makes me ☺ ?

What am I thankful for?

Sweet Ass Ideas for:

- -

What are the two **most valuable freedom actions** I will take today to progress toward my vision, goals, and dream life?

1.

2.

What will I **give** and/or **minimize** today?

My **wins** for the day are:

I have an **abundance** of:

What are the two **most valuable freedom actions** I will take tomorrow to progress toward my vision, goals, and dream life?

1.

2.

Nightly Affirmations, I am…

Did I accomplish my two main freedom actions today?　☺ 😐 ☹

Did I give a gift and/or minimize?　☺ 😐 ☹

What was it and how did it feel? _____

I meditated for .... minutes today and I felt: _____

You are　**73**% done with developing your happiness muscle :)

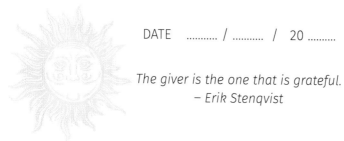

DATE .... / .... / 20 ....

The giver is the one that is grateful.
– Erik Stenqvist

What makes me ☺ ?

What am I thankful for?

Sweet Ass Ideas for:

What are the two **most valuable freedom actions** I will take today to progress toward my vision, goals, and dream life?

1.

2.

What will I **give** and/or **minimize** today?

My **wins** for the day are:

I have an **abundance** of:

What are the two **most valuable freedom actions** I will take tomorrow to progress toward my vision, goals, and dream life?

1.

2.

Nightly Affirmations, I am…

Did I accomplish my two main freedom actions today? ☺ ☺ ☹

Did I give a gift and/or minimize? ☺ ☺ ☹

What was it and how did it feel? _____

I meditated for .... **minutes today and I felt:** _____

You are **74**% done with developing your happiness muscle :)

DATE .... / .... / 20 ....

If you stay loyal to your passion, you will live the life of your dreams.
If you don't, there's no way you can.
— Dave Lent

What makes me ☺ ?

What am I thankful for?

Sweet Ass Ideas for:

- -

What are the two **most valuable freedom actions** I will take today to progress toward my vision, goals, and dream life?

1.

2.

What will I **give** and/or **minimize** today?

My **wins** for the day are:

I have an **abundance** of:

What are the two **most valuable freedom actions** I will take tomorrow to progress toward my vision, goals, and dream life?

1.

2.

Nightly Affirmations, I am...

Did I accomplish my two main freedom actions today? ☺ ☺ ☹

Did I give a gift and/or minimize? ☺ ☺ ☹

What was it and how did it feel? _____

I meditated for .... **minutes today and I felt:** _____

You are **75**% done with developing your happiness muscle :)

DATE .... / .... / 20 ....

Avoid being boxed in. Go find something that allows you to breathe.
—Bri Seeley

What makes me ☺ ?

What am I thankful for?

Sweet Ass Ideas for:

- -

What are the two **most valuable freedom actions** I will take today to progress toward my vision, goals, and dream life?

1.

2.

What will I **give** and/or **minimize** today?

My **wins** for the day are:

I have an **abundance** of:

What are the two **most valuable freedom actions** I will take tomorrow to progress toward my vision, goals, and dream life?

1.

2.

Nightly Affirmations, I am...

Did I accomplish my two main freedom actions today? ☺ ☺ ☹

Did I give a gift and/or minimize? ☺ ☺ ☹

What was it and how did it feel? _____

I meditated for .... minutes today and I felt: _____

You are **76** % done with developing your happiness muscle :)

DATE .... / .... / 20 ....

Why do we humans lock ourselves in cages, at our desks,
while no other species is doing it?
—Fabian Dittrich

What makes me ☺ ?

What am I thankful for?

Sweet Ass Ideas for:

- -

What are the two **most valuable freedom actions** I will take today to progress toward my vision, goals, and dream life?

1.

2.

What will I **give** and/or **minimize** today?

My **wins** for the day are:

I have an **abundance** of:

What are the two **most valuable freedom actions** I will take tomorrow to progress toward my vision, goals, and dream life?

1.

2.

Nightly Affirmations, I am...

Did I accomplish my two main freedom actions today? ☺ ☻ ☹

Did I give a gift and/or minimize? ☺ ☻ ☹

What was it and how did it feel? _____

I meditated for .... **minutes today and I felt:** _____

You are   **77**% done with developing your happiness muscle :)

DATE .... / .... / 20 ....

The perfect is the enemy of the good.
—Orlando Pescetti

What makes me ☺ ?

What am I thankful for?

Sweet Ass Ideas for:

What are the two **most valuable freedom actions** I will take today to progress toward my vision, goals, and dream life?

1.

2.

What will I **give** and/or **minimize** today?

My **wins** for the day are:

I have an **abundance** of:

What are the two **most valuable freedom actions** I will take tomorrow to progress toward my vision, goals, and dream life?

1.

2.

Nightly Affirmations, I am...

Did I accomplish my two main freedom actions today? ☺ ☻ ☹

Did I give a gift and/or minimize? ☺ ☻ ☹

What was it and how did it feel? _____

I meditated for .... **minutes today and I felt:** _____

You are **78**% done with developing your happiness muscle :)

DATE .... / .... / 20 ....

If you keep going, keep working, keep believing — success is guaranteed. Dare to dream.
—Jacqueline du Plessis

What makes me ☺ ?

What am I thankful for?

Sweet Ass Ideas for:

- -

What are the two **most valuable freedom actions** I will take today to progress toward my vision, goals, and dream life?

1.

2.

What will I **give** and/or **minimize** today?

My **wins** for the day are:

I have an **abundance** of:

What are the two **most valuable freedom actions** I will take tomorrow
to progress toward my vision, goals, and dream life?

1.

2.

Nightly Affirmations, I am...

Did I accomplish my two main freedom actions today? ☺ 😐 ☹

Did I give a gift and/or minimize? ☺ 😐 ☹

What was it and how did it feel? _____

I meditated for .... **minutes today and I felt:** _____

DATE .... / .... / 20 ....

We have to trust our instincts, honor them,
and move forward despite what everybody says.
– Cynthia Miltenberger

What makes me ☺ ?

What am I thankful for?

Sweet Ass Ideas for:

- -

What are the two **most valuable freedom actions** I will take today to progress toward my vision, goals, and dream life?

1.

2.

What will I **give** and/or **minimize** today?

My **wins** for the day are:

I have an **abundance** of:

What are the two **most valuable freedom actions** I will take tomorrow to progress toward my vision, goals, and dream life?

1.

2.

Nightly Affirmations, I am...

Did I accomplish my two main freedom actions today? ☺ 😐 ☹

Did I give a gift and/or minimize? ☺ 😐 ☹

What was it and how did it feel? _____

I meditated for .... **minutes today and I felt:** _____

You are **80** % done with developing your happiness muscle :)

DATE .... / .... / 20 ....

We have this idea that there are only two choices in life:
1.) Get a job or 2.) Starve. There are a lot more options in this life.
– Jeff Steinmann

What makes me ☺ ?

What am I thankful for?

Sweet Ass Ideas for:

- -

What are the two **most valuable freedom actions** I will take today to progress toward my vision, goals, and dream life?

1.

2.

What will I **give** and/or **minimize** today?

My **wins** for the day are:

I have an **abundance** of:

What are the two **most valuable freedom actions** I will take tomorrow to progress toward my vision, goals, and dream life?

1.

2.

Nightly Affirmations, I am...

Did I accomplish my two main freedom actions today? ☺ ☺ ☹

Did I give a gift and/or minimize? ☺ ☺ ☹

What was it and how did it feel? _____

I meditated for .... **minutes today and I felt:** _____

DATE .... / .... / 20 ....

A bird in hand is worth two in the bush.
– John Ray

What makes me ☺ ?

What am I thankful for?

Sweet Ass Ideas for:

- -

What are the two **most valuable freedom actions** I will take today to progress toward my vision, goals, and dream life?

1.

2.

What will I **give** and/or **minimize** today?

My **wins** for the day are:

I have an **abundance** of:

What are the two **most valuable freedom actions** I will take tomorrow to progress toward my vision, goals, and dream life?

1.

2.

Nightly Affirmations, I am…

Did I accomplish my two main freedom actions today? ☺ ☺ ☹

Did I give a gift and/or minimize? ☺ ☺ ☹

What was it and how did it feel? _____

I meditated for …………… minutes today and I felt: _____

You are **82**% done with developing your happiness muscle :)

Every single day of our life is a precious moment, and we have no guarantees on how many of these we will have.
– Jeena Cho

What makes me ☺ ?

What am I thankful for?

Sweet Ass Ideas for:

- -

What are the two **most valuable freedom actions** I will take today to progress toward my vision, goals, and dream life?

1.

2.

What will I **give** and/or **minimize** today?

My **wins** for the day are:

I have an **abundance** of:

What are the two **most valuable freedom actions** I will take tomorrow to progress toward my vision, goals, and dream life?

1.

2.

Nightly Affirmations, I am...

Did I accomplish my two main freedom actions today? ☺ 😐 ☹

Did I give a gift and/or minimize? ☺ 😐 ☹

What was it and how did it feel? _____

I meditated for .... **minutes today and I felt:** _____

You are **83**% done with developing your happiness muscle :)

DATE .... / .... / 20 ....

There will always be problems, which means there is always opportunity to creatively solve these problems. Freedom is for those who solve the problems. – Heath Armstrong

What makes me ☺ ?

What am I thankful for?

Sweet Ass Ideas for:

- -

What are the two **most valuable freedom actions** I will take today to progress toward my vision, goals, and dream life?

1.

2.

What will I **give** and/or **minimize** today?

My **wins** for the day are:

I have an **abundance** of:

What are the two **most valuable freedom actions** I will take tomorrow
to progress toward my vision, goals, and dream life?

1.

2.

Nightly Affirmations, I am…

Did I accomplish my two main freedom actions today? ☺ ☻ ☹

Did I give a gift and/or minimize? ☺ ☻ ☹

What was it and how did it feel? _____

I meditated for .... **minutes today and I felt:** _____

You are **84**% done with developing your happiness muscle :)

DATE ………… / ………… / 20 …………

If you keep succeeding at everything, life will just be boring.
– Tony Barber

What makes me ☺ ?

What am I thankful for?

Sweet Ass Ideas for:

- -

What are the two **most valuable freedom actions** I will take today to progress toward my vision, goals, and dream life?

1.

2.

What will I **give** and/or **minimize** today?

My **wins** for the day are:

I have an **abundance** of:

What are the two **most valuable freedom actions** I will take tomorrow to progress toward my vision, goals, and dream life?

1.

2.

Nightly Affirmations, I am...

Did I accomplish my two main freedom actions today? ☺ 😐 ☹

Did I give a gift and/or minimize? ☺ 😐 ☹

What was it and how did it feel? _____

I meditated for .... **minutes today and I felt:** _____

You are **85 %** done with developing your happiness muscle :)

DATE .... / .... / 20 ....

The universe is like water. You can swim through it,
you just have to pick a direction and go with it.
— Jason Berwick

What makes me ☺ ?

What am I thankful for?

Sweet Ass Ideas for:

What are the two **most valuable freedom actions** I will take today to progress toward my vision, goals, and dream life?

1.

2.

What will I **give** and/or **minimize** today?

My **wins** for the day are:

I have an **abundance** of:

What are the two **most valuable freedom actions** I will take tomorrow to progress toward my vision, goals, and dream life?

1.

2.

Nightly Affirmations, I am...

Did I accomplish my two main freedom actions today?   ☺ ☺ ☹

Did I give a gift and/or minimize?   ☺ ☺ ☹

What was it and how did it feel? _____

I meditated for .... **minutes today and I felt:** _____

You are   **86**% done with developing your happiness muscle :)

DATE .... / .... / 20 ....

You can have everything in life you want if you will just help enough people get what they want.
– Zig Ziglar

What makes me ☺ ?

What am I thankful for?

Sweet Ass Ideas for:

- -

What are the two **most valuable freedom actions** I will take today to progress toward my vision, goals, and dream life?

1.

2.

What will I **give** and/or **minimize** today?

My **wins** for the day are:

I have an **abundance** of:

What are the two **most valuable freedom actions** I will take tomorrow to progress toward my vision, goals, and dream life?

1.

2.

Nightly Affirmations, I am...

Did I accomplish my two main freedom actions today? ☺ ☺ ☹

Did I give a gift and/or minimize? ☺ ☺ ☹

What was it and how did it feel? _____

I meditated for .... **minutes today and I felt:** _____

You are **87**% done with developing your happiness muscle :)

DATE .... / .... / 20 ....

Start making decisions based on who you want to be,
not on who you are right now.
– Amber Ludwig-Vilhauer

What makes me ☺ ?

What am I thankful for?

Sweet Ass Ideas for:

- -

What are the two **most valuable freedom actions** I will take today to progress toward my vision, goals, and dream life?

1.

2.

What will I **give** and/or **minimize** today?

My **wins** for the day are:

I have an **abundance** of:

What are the two **most valuable freedom actions** I will take tomorrow to progress toward my vision, goals, and dream life?

1.

2.

Nightly Affirmations, I am...

Did I accomplish my two main freedom actions today? ☺ ☺ ☹

Did I give a gift and/or minimize? ☺ ☺ ☹

What was it and how did it feel? _____

I meditated for .... **minutes today and I felt:** _____

You are **88**% done with developing your happiness muscle :)

DATE .... / .... / 20 ....

Mindfulness leads to the discovery of your true essence.
– Molly Knight Forde

What makes me ☺ ?

What am I thankful for?

Sweet Ass Ideas for:

What are the two **most valuable freedom actions** I will take today to progress toward my vision, goals, and dream life?

1.

2.

What will I **give** and/or **minimize** today?

My **wins** for the day are:

I have an **abundance** of:

What are the two **most valuable freedom actions** I will take tomorrow to progress toward my vision, goals, and dream life?

1.

2.

Nightly Affirmations, I am…

Did I accomplish my two main freedom actions today? ☺ ☺ ☹

Did I give a gift and/or minimize? ☺ ☺ ☹

What was it and how did it feel? _____

I meditated for .... **minutes today and I felt:** _____

You are **89**% done with developing your happiness muscle :)

DATE .... / .... / 20 ....

You are your own lottery ticket. If you invest in yourself and take some risks, you will create the life of your dreams.
– Heath Armstrong

What makes me ☺ ?

What am I thankful for?

Sweet Ass Ideas for:

- -

What are the two **most valuable freedom actions** I will take today to progress toward my vision, goals, and dream life?

1.

2.

What will I **give** and/or **minimize** today?

My **wins** for the day are:

I have an **abundance** of:

What are the two **most valuable freedom actions** I will take tomorrow to progress toward my vision, goals, and dream life?

1.

2.

Nightly Affirmations, I am...

Did I accomplish my two main freedom actions today? ☺ ☺ ☹

Did I give a gift and/or minimize? ☺ ☺ ☹

What was it and how did it feel? _____

I meditated for .... **minutes today and I felt:** _____

You are **90**% done with developing your happiness muscle :)

You can punch a wall or write a song. Just as painful either way, but you have something to show for it at the end of the day with a song.
– Trent Reznor

What makes me ☺ ?

What am I thankful for?

Sweet Ass Ideas for:

What are the two **most valuable freedom actions** I will take today to progress toward my vision, goals, and dream life?

1.

2.

What will I **give** and/or **minimize** today?

My **wins** for the day are:

I have an **abundance** of:

What are the two **most valuable freedom actions** I will take tomorrow
to progress toward my vision, goals, and dream life?

1.

2.

Nightly Affirmations, I am...

Did I accomplish my two main freedom actions today? ☺ ☻ ☹

Did I give a gift and/or minimize? ☺ ☻ ☹

What was it and how did it feel? _____

I meditated for .... **minutes today and I felt:** _____

You are **91%** done with developing your happiness muscle :)

DATE .... / .... / 20 ....

Go to the meadows. Go to the garden. Go to the woods. Open your eyes!
– Albert Hoffman

What makes me ☺ ?

What am I thankful for?

Sweet Ass Ideas for:

- -

What are the two **most valuable freedom actions** I will take today to progress toward my vision, goals, and dream life?

1.

2.

What will I **give** and/or **minimize** today?

My **wins** for the day are:

I have an **abundance** of:

What are the two **most valuable freedom actions** I will take tomorrow to progress toward my vision, goals, and dream life?

1.

2.

Nightly Affirmations, I am...

Did I accomplish my two main freedom actions today? ☺ ☺ ☹

Did I give a gift and/or minimize? ☺ ☺ ☹

What was it and how did it feel? _____

I meditated for .... minutes today and I felt: _____

You are **92** % done with developing your happiness muscle :)

DATE .... / .... / 20 ....

The purpose of truly transcendent art is to express something you are not yet, but something that you can become.
– Alex Grey

What makes me ☺ ?

What am I thankful for?

Sweet Ass Ideas for:

What are the two **most valuable freedom actions** I will take today to progress toward my vision, goals, and dream life?

1.

2.

What will I **give** and/or **minimize** today?

My **wins** for the day are:

I have an **abundance** of:

What are the two **most valuable freedom actions** I will take tomorrow to progress toward my vision, goals, and dream life?

1.

2.

Nightly Affirmations, I am...

Did I accomplish my two main freedom actions today? ☺ 😐 ☹

Did I give a gift and/or minimize? ☺ 😐 ☹

What was it and how did it feel? _____

I meditated for .... **minutes today and I felt:** _____

You are   93% done with developing your happiness muscle :)

DATE .... / .... / 20 ....

Children are smarter than any of us. Know how I know that?
I don't know one child with a full time job.
— Bill Hicks

What makes me ☺ ?

What am I thankful for?

Sweet Ass Ideas for:

- -

What are the two **most valuable freedom actions** I will take today to progress toward my vision, goals, and dream life?

1.

2.

What will I **give** and/or **minimize** today?

My **wins** for the day are:

I have an **abundance** of:

What are the two **most valuable freedom actions** I will take tomorrow to progress toward my vision, goals, and dream life?

1.

2.

Nightly Affirmations, I am...

Did I accomplish my two main freedom actions today? ☺ 😐 ☹

Did I give a gift and/or minimize? ☺ 😐 ☹

What was it and how did it feel? _____

I meditated for .... **minutes today and I felt:** _____

You are   **94**% done with developing your happiness muscle :)

DATE .... / .... / 20 ....

You've got to take risks if you're going to succeed.
I would much rather ask forgiveness than permission.
– Richard Branson

What makes me ☺ ?

What am I thankful for?

Sweet Ass Ideas for:

What are the two **most valuable freedom actions** I will take today to progress toward my vision, goals, and dream life?

1.

2.

What will I **give** and/or **minimize** today?

My **wins** for the day are:

I have an **abundance** of:

What are the two **most valuable freedom actions** I will take tomorrow to progress toward my vision, goals, and dream life?

1.

2.

Nightly Affirmations, I am...

Did I accomplish my two main freedom actions today? ☺ ☺ ☹

Did I give a gift and/or minimize? ☺ ☺ ☹

What was it and how did it feel? _____

I meditated for .... minutes today and I felt: _____

You are **95**% done with developing your happiness muscle :)

DATE ……… / ……… / 20 ………

It's easy to be miserable. Being happy is tougher — and cooler.
— Thom Yorke

What makes me ☺ ?

What am I thankful for?

Sweet Ass Ideas for:

- -

What are the two **most valuable freedom actions** I will take today to progress toward my vision, goals, and dream life?

1.

2.

What will I **give** and/or **minimize** today?

My **wins** for the day are:

I have an **abundance** of:

What are the two **most valuable freedom actions** I will take tomorrow to progress toward my vision, goals, and dream life?

1.

2.

Nightly Affirmations, I am...

Did I accomplish my two main freedom actions today? ☺ ☺ ☹

Did I give a gift and/or minimize? ☺ ☺ ☹

What was it and how did it feel? _____

I meditated for .... **minutes today and I felt:** _____

You are **96** % done with developing your happiness muscle :)

DATE ………… / ………… / 20 ………

If you don't have a plan, you become part of somebody else's plan.
– Terence McKenna

What makes me ☺ ?

What am I thankful for?

Sweet Ass Ideas for:

- -

What are the two **most valuable freedom actions** I will take today to progress toward my vision, goals, and dream life?

1.

2.

What will I **give** and/or **minimize** today?

My **wins** for the day are:

I have an **abundance** of:

What are the two **most valuable freedom actions** I will take tomorrow to progress toward my vision, goals, and dream life?

1.

2.

Nightly Affirmations, I am...

Did I accomplish my two main freedom actions today? ☺ ☺ ☹

Did I give a gift and/or minimize? ☺ ☺ ☹

What was it and how did it feel? _____

I meditated for .... minutes today and I felt: _____

You are **97**% done with developing your happiness muscle :)

I used to live in a room full of mirrors; all I could see was me. I take my spirit and I crash my mirrors; now the whole world is here for me to see.
– Jimi Hendrix

What makes me ☺ ?

What am I thankful for?

Sweet Ass Ideas for:

What are the two **most valuable freedom actions** I will take today to progress toward my vision, goals, and dream life?

1.

2.

What will I **give** and/or **minimize** today?

My **wins** for the day are:

I have an **abundance** of:

What are the two **most valuable freedom actions** I will take tomorrow to progress toward my vision, goals, and dream life?

1.

2.

Nightly Affirmations, I am...

Did I accomplish my two main freedom actions today? ☺ ☺ ☹

Did I give a gift and/or minimize? ☺ ☺ ☹

What was it and how did it feel? _____

I meditated for .... **minutes today and I felt:** _____

You are **98**% done with developing your happiness muscle :)

DATE .... / .... / 20 ....

Most folks are as happy as they make up their minds to be.
– Abraham Lincoln

What makes me ☺ ?

What am I thankful for?

Sweet Ass Ideas for:

What are the two **most valuable freedom actions** I will take today to progress toward my vision, goals, and dream life?

1.

2.

What will I **give** and/or **minimize** today?

My **wins** for the day are:

I have an **abundance** of:

What are the two **most valuable freedom actions** I will take tomorrow to progress toward my vision, goals, and dream life?

1.

2.

Nightly Affirmations, I am...

Did I accomplish my two main freedom actions today? ☺ ☺ ☹

Did I give a gift and/or minimize? ☺ ☺ ☹

What was it and how did it feel? _____

I meditated for .... **minutes today and I felt:** _____

You are   **99**% done with developing your happiness muscle :)

DATE .... / .... / 20 ....

Don't cry because it's over. Smile because it happened.
– Dr. Seuss

What makes me ☺ ?

What am I thankful for?

Sweet Ass Ideas for:

What are the two **most valuable freedom actions** I will take today to progress toward my vision, goals, and dream life?

1.

2.

What will I **give** and/or **minimize** today?

My **wins** for the day are:

I have an **abundance** of:

What are the two **most valuable freedom actions** I will take tomorrow to progress toward my vision, goals, and dream life?

1.

2.

Nightly Affirmations, I am...

Did I accomplish my two main freedom actions today? ☺ ☺ ☹

Did I give a gift and/or minimize? ☺ ☺ ☹

What was it and how did it feel? _____

I meditated for .... **minutes today and I felt:** _____

You are **100** % done with developing your happiness muscle :)

Sweet Ass Finish Line

YEAAAAAAAAAAA! YOU DID IT! You beautiful maniac! You slaughtered your resistance gremlins and left them to rot in a big smelly pile of dung that even the ass of a dead rhino couldn't top.

How does it feel? After 100 days of carving your foundation for happiness, what has changed in your life? Did the freedom buds you set at the beginning of the journey manifest? Take a moment to sit back and reflect on the last 100 days of journaling, and notice the difference between the person you are now, and the person you were when you started.

Your spaceship is on full throttle. You have tasted the power of visualization, meditation, positivity, gratitude, brainstorming, focus, celebration, and reflection! You have eliminated distractions and gifted the Universe, and in return, the Universe is gifting you! Go back through your journal and read your entries. That warm fuzzy feeling will overwhelm you. Notice the people you have touched through the kindness of your gifts, and also the acceleration and growth of your wins!

Your happiness muscle is in full beast mode, and it's ready for some more juice, but it's important to reward yourself for your accomplishment! Do something you've always wanted to do. Skydiving? Backpacking across another country? Pogo-sticking across the neighborhood in your undies? Anything! (I will not take responsibility if you get arrested for pogo sticking in your undies.)

I am proud of you, not only because you joined the freedom army and won this battle against the resistance gremlins, but because you supported and fought for your wild, crazy, and "unrealistic" dreams. I respect you and salute you. You have created a habit that will exponentially grow into infinite happiness, freedom, and purpose in life if you keep working it out! And, whether you realize it or not, the energy of your transformation has directly planted seeds in others around you to awaken their own happiness muscle and create the life they love.

I would love to hear from you about your experience with this journal and practice. When I first created this process for myself, I never imagined it would be something I would share with others. It is my great honor to share this part of me with you, and I hope you will take a few moments to share your experience with me. You can email me at **heath@fistpumps.com** (selfies only allowed if you are holding a sign that says *"I slaughter resistance gremlins"* and you have your pants on) or join the Facebook group and meet the other soldiers by accessing the resource links at:

www.sweetassjournal.com/bonus

Soon, the gremlins will plan another disco party bonanza with you as the host, but you will be more ready than ever to squash them like grapes with your Arnold Schwarzenegger-like muscles of happiness.

You are a freedom warrior, and I'll be right here with you.

The next 100 days starts tomorrow! Let's rage!

Special Invitation to Connect

If you found value in this journal and practice, consider gifting it to family members, friends, and co-workers. It's always magical to watch the domino effect! If you want multiple copies, please hit me up via email, and I'll give you a bulk discount!

Don't forget to take advantage of the free bonus material if you haven't already at *www.sweetassjournal.com/bonus*

If you are interested in being a part of my advanced reading team for future publications (The Gremlin Smasher Review Team), I'd love to have you join the group! I'll be posting free and discounted future products in exchange for your honest opinions! You can also connect with others and share your experience with the journal. There is nothing that has been more valuable than connecting with other like-minded individuals in my life. I look forward to meeting you! The link to the closed Facebook group is also in the bonus sections! I only accept friend requests from people who are wearing pants!

Cheerios!

Acknowledgements

First, I'd like to thank the magical Universe for seeding my mind with infinite ideas and opportunities, and for gifting me with the most loving and supportive parents and sisters anyone could ask for. Big ups to my awesome Grandparents as well for supporting all of us. I am the sum total of all of you.

To my gorgeous sidekick and fiancee Lindsay for being my never-ending energy source, and for being the first person to show me how to remove my boundaries and do awesome shit ALL THE TIME. You are my nature companion and I love you more than Arnold Schwarzenegger.

To Jacqueline du Plessis for teaching me how to slow down and focus on what matters in life. You taught me that life is as infinite as we allow it to be.

To Jason Berwick for teaching me e-commerce and being the only other absolute raging maniac who thinks life is a video game and money is fake. Special thanks for not dying 11 miles deep in Snoqualmie. There are too many levels left to beat.

I also want to give a special thanks to all of my teachers, mentors, and influences that have impacted me throughout my journey: Jared Angaza, Amber Ludwig-Vilhauer, Honoree Corder, Paul Kemp, Kim Nicol, Dave Lent, Hal Elrod, Jason Moore, Chris Guillebeau, Tom Corson Knowles, Dan Norris, Trajan King, Jeena Cho, Nick Such, Steve P. Young, Shawn Stevenson, Joshua Fields Millburn, Ryan Nicodemus, Erik Stenqvist, and Ed Heller.

And finally, a big hug to my team and my assistants who hold my hand in the trenches. I wouldn't be here without you Alyssa, Riley, Lindsay, Mina, Judy, Fenny, Dannah, Cliff, Lily and Patty-Mack.

Sweet Ass Author Bio

I'm Heath Armstrong. My life mission is to help motivate you to destroy the fear gremlins that hold your freedom and super-powers hostage. My passion is teaching skills and techniques to help you beast up your happiness muscles and build your empire of smiles. To defeat my own dark villains, I spent 200+ hours interviewing over 100 creative masterminds on the magic behind transforming visions to reality. In the process, I sold my house and everything I owned to eliminate distractions and debt, and I eventually retired my 'career' for full-time location independence and entrepreneurship. In 2015, I started an e-commerce company that has sold over $1.3 million in sweet ass products to date, and I only work around 2 hours/day on this business. My latest projects include The Sweet Ass Journal to Develop Your Happiness Muscle in 100 Days, and The Sweet Ass Domination Deck to Motivate Your Maniac Creative Mind.

Follow me on social media @heathfistpumps
Also check out The Never Stop Peaking Podcast on iTunes / Stitcher
The Sweet Ass Domination Deck at RageCreate.com
HeathArmstrong.com

Made in the USA
Middletown, DE
24 November 2020

24957816R00170